RURAL REVITALIZATION IN CHINA

中国乡村振兴报告

（国际版）

农业农村部农村经济研究中心　主编

中国出版集团有限公司

研究出版社

图书在版编目（CIP）数据

中国乡村振兴报告：国际版 / 农业农村部农村经济
研究中心主编. -- 北京：研究出版社，2024.12
ISBN 978-7-5199-1429-5

Ⅰ. ①中… Ⅱ. ①农… Ⅲ. ①农村 - 社会主义建设 -
研究报告 - 中国 Ⅳ. ①F320.3

中国国家版本馆CIP数据核字（2023）第034005号

出 品 人：陈建军
出版统筹：丁　波
责任编辑：寇颖丹

中国乡村振兴报告：国际版

ZHONGGUO XIANGCUN ZHENXING BAOGAO: GUOJI BAN
农业农村部农村经济研究中心　主编
研究出版社 出版发行
（100006　北京市东城区灯市口大街100号华腾商务楼）
北京中科印刷有限公司印刷　新华书店经销
2024年12月第1版　2024年12月第1次印刷
开本：710毫米 × 1000毫米　1/16　印张：12
字数：115千字
ISBN 978-7-5199-1429-5　定价：68.00元
电话（010）64217619　64217652（发行部）

前言

党的十九大报告中首次提出实施乡村振兴战略，并作为七大战略之一写入中国共产党章程。在这之后，连续五年的中央一号文件都重点围绕实现乡村产业、人才、文化、生态、组织振兴五个方面来制定目标、部署政策，全面谋划新时代乡村全面振兴的顶层设计。除此之外，2018年国家专门出台并推进实施相配套的《乡村振兴战略规划（2018—2022年）》，明确了2020年全面建成小康社会和2022年召开党的二十大时乡村振兴战略的阶段性目标任务，细化相应的工作重点和政策措施。

贯彻落实中央一号文件部署要求，实施乡村振兴战略的投入要素支持保障方面，2020年中共中央办公厅、国务院办公厅印发《关于调整完善土地出让收入使用范围优先支持乡村振兴的意见》，对开拓乡村振兴资金筹措渠道、建立财政投入稳定增长的长效机制、提高土地出让收入用于农业农村的比例，作出了专门的制度安排。2021年，中国人民银行和中国银行保险监督管理委员会联合出台《金融机构服务乡村振兴考核评估办法》，以考核评估指挥棒，督促引导更多金融资源配置到农村经济社会发展的重点领域和薄弱环节，对金融资源加大乡村振兴支持力度作出专门部署。

乡村振兴战略工作机制建设方面，国家层面推动实施乡村振兴战略领导责任制，实行中央统筹省负总责市县抓落实的工作机制，规定省及以下各级党政一把手是乡村振兴战略的第一责任人，实行五级书记抓乡村振兴，县委书记是县域乡村振兴的"一线总指挥"。组织开展省级党政领导班子和领导干部推进乡村振兴战略实绩考核，建立起市县党政领导班子和党政干部推进乡村振兴战略实绩考核制度，谋划推进乡村振兴责任制实施办法。每年各省（区、市）党委和政府向党中央国务院报告推进乡村振兴战略的进展情况，中央农村工作领导小组办公室牵头对各地各部门落实中央一号文件和乡村振兴战略情况开展年度督查。

制度和法律法规保障方面，2019年和2021年分别出台的《中国共产党农村工作条例》和《中华人民共和国乡村振兴促进法》，把这些年关于脱贫攻坚和乡村振兴战略行之有效的政策体系、工作机制和工作方法等，以党内法规和法律形式固定下来。至此，随着乡村振兴战略系列配套政策文件陆续出台，现今国家层面上乡村振兴战略的"四梁八柱"式制度框架和政策体系已初步健全，工作机制和抓手也不断完善，为农业农村现代化建设打好了基础。

过去五年，中国农业农村发展取得了历史性成就、发生了历史性变革。国家粮食安全保障水平进一步提高。粮食生产持续稳定在1.3万亿斤的高点平台，2021年我国人均粮食占有量达到483公斤，显著超过国际平均水平。现代农业体系构建和农业高质量发展成就斐然。农业科技贡献率超过60%，主要农作物耕种收综合机械化率超过73%，基本实现良种全覆盖。多种形式适度规模经营加快发展。家庭农场、农民合作社、龙头企业等新型农业经营主体蓬勃成长，新型规模经营主体总数量超过660万家。农业绿色发展迈出坚实步伐。耕地保护、节水灌溉、农业资源保护利用全面进展，全国耕地质量平均等级比2014年提高0.35个等级，2018年以来每年发展节水灌溉2000万亩以上，畜禽粪污综合利用率超过76%，秸秆综合利用率超过86%，农膜回收率达到80%，农作物化肥农药施用量连续5年负增长。农民收入水平进一步提高，脱贫攻坚成果得到进一步巩固。现行标准下的9899万贫困人口成功实现脱贫，与全国人民一道进入小康社会。截至2023年，近70%的监测对象已消除返贫致贫风险，剩余监测对象均已安排有针对性的帮扶措施。农村居民收入持续较快增长，城乡居民收入比持续下降到2021年的2.5∶1。农村人居环境得到明显改善。农村人居环境整治三年行动方案目标任务全面完成。2018年以来，全国累计改造农村户厕4000多万户，全国农村卫生厕所普及率超过70%，农村生活垃圾进行收运处理的自然村比例稳定保持在90%以上，农村生活污水治理率达到25.5%。农村生活基础设施大幅改善，全国具备条件的乡镇、建制村100%通硬化路、100%通客车，全国农村自来水普及率达到84%。全国各地建成了超过5万个各种类型的美丽宜居乡村。

纵观改革开放40多年，作为最大的发展中国家，中国在推进快速工业化和城镇化过程中，成功避免了农业萎缩、农村凋敝、农民贫困的发展陷阱。尤其是党的十九大以来，乡村振兴战略的实施，使我国农业农村发展受重视程度和被支持力度不断提高，农村越来越快速、越来越接近跟上城镇的发展步伐。中国实施乡村振兴战略经验、中国方案和智慧，对同样在探索农村发展路径的广大发展中国家，将提供有益参考。

目录

总　论

一、研究背景

面对日益严峻的环境保护形势和新时代人类包容性增长的迫切需要，2015年联合国通过了2030年可持续发展议程，并公布了17项全球可持续发展目标（SDGs）。在国际社会多年的共同努力下，人类在减少饥饿与贫困、提高人类发展水平等诸多方面取得了显著成就。然而，新冠疫情的暴发使多年取得的发展成就出现逆转，根据《人类发展报告2021/2022》显示，全球人类发展指数自采用以来首次出现连续两年下降的情况，确立可持续发展目标以来所取得的大部分进展均被逆转。[①]加上战争冲突和逐渐频发的气候灾害等多重因素冲击，使得更多的脆弱人群重新面临贫困、饥饿、流离失所等问题，加剧了全球的不平等。全球经历的疫情、能源及气候危机均对相对弱势的农村群体产生显著影响，如何在这个复杂背景下支持乡村的可持续发展、保护乡村居民的生计是一个世界性的议题。

---

① 联合国：全球人类发展指数连续两年倒退，https://mp.weixin.qq.com/s?__biz=MjM5NzU4OTM0MQ==&mid=2651082206&idx=1&sn=5603663f4150fb1cb0221a835860ef1e&chksm=bd2755ec8a50dcfac33612b5fdce3f737e4d7da9afa5293e3bf95dee52e78-c2917556304e29e&scene=27，2022-09-11。
央视网：联合国最新《人类发展报告》发布，全球发展不均衡现象加剧，https://news.cctv.cn/2024/03/15/ARTIMxhXnXGM8A8OSxfroY7b240315.shtml，2024-03-15。

为了更好地支持农村发展、缩小中国长期存在的城乡差距，中国在2017年提出了乡村振兴战略，从多个维度实施政策上的主动干预，在消除贫困、确保粮食安全、保障基本公共服务、缩小城乡差距、抵御自然灾害、推动绿色可持续发展等方面都取得积极成效。不仅推动了SDG1无贫困、SDG2零饥饿和SDG10减少不平等的进程，也对其他领域的相关SDG起到了积极的贡献作用（表1尝试梳理了乡村振兴战略规划主要指标与SDGs的对应关系）。作为全世界最大的发展中国家，中国对于其他发展中国家具有示范作用。因此，本报告将对中国乡村振兴的实践及经验进行梳理，向世界全面客观地介绍当代中国在促进农村发展方面的政策安排及成果，为世界特别是发展中国家解决"三农"问题贡献中国智慧和中国方案。

表1　乡村振兴战略规划主要指标与SDGs的对应关系分析

分类	主要指标	对应的SDG指标
产业兴旺	1.粮食综合生产能力	SDG2
	2.农业科技进步贡献率	SDG2
	3.农业劳动生产率	SDG2
	4.农产品加工产值与农业总产值比	SDG2
	5.休闲农业和乡村旅游接待人次	SDG8
生态宜居	6.畜禽粪污综合利用率	SDG12
	7.村庄绿化覆盖率	SDG15
	8.对生活垃圾进行处理的村占比	SDG6
	9.农村卫生厕所普及率	SDG6

续表

分类	主要指标	对应的SDG指标
乡风文明	10.村综合性文化服务中心覆盖率	SDG8
	11.县级及以上文明村和乡镇占比	SDG8
	12.农村义务教育学校专任教师本科以上学历比例	SDG4
	13.农村居民教育文化娱乐支出占比	SDG4
治理有效	14.村庄规划管理覆盖率	SDG11
	15.建有综合服务站的村占比	SDG16
	16.村党组织书记兼任村委会主任的村占比	无
	17.有村规民约的村占比	无
	18.集体经济强村比重	SDG8
生活富裕	19.农村居民恩格尔系数	SDG1
	20.城乡居民收入比	SDG10
	21.农村自来水普及率	SDG6
	22.具备条件的建制村通硬化路比例	SDG9

注：SDG1：在全世界消除一切形式的贫困；SDG2：消除饥饿，实现粮食安全，改善营养状况和促进可持续农业；SDG4：确保包容和公平的优质教育，让全民终身享有学习机会；SDG6：为所有人提供水和环境卫生并对其进行可持续管理；SDG8：促进持久、包容和可持续经济增长，促进充分的生产性就业和人人获得体面工作；SDG9：建造具备抵御灾害能力的基础设施，促进可持续工业化和推动创新；SDG10：减少国家内部和国家之间的不平等；SDG11：建设包容、安全、有抵御灾害能力和可持续的城市和人类社区；SDG12：采用可持续的消费和生产模式；SDG15：保护、恢复和促进可持续利用陆地生态系统、可持续森林管理、防治荒漠化、制止和扭转土地退化现象、遏制生物多样性的丧失；SDG16：创建和平、包容的社会以促进可持续发展，让所有人都能诉诸司法，在各级建立有效、负责和包容的机构。表中对应关系为分析得出，部分指标可能存在多个对应关系，这里只标明主要的。

二、乡村振兴战略

（一）乡村振兴战略的提出

中国是拥有14亿人口、世界上最大的发展中国家，过去曾饱受贫困问题的困扰。针对贫困问题，中国政府积极推进精准扶贫，在精准识别贫困人群及其致贫原因的基础之上，有针对性地采取一揽子帮扶措施，并投入大量的人力及财力。截至2020年底，中国如期完成新时代脱贫攻坚目标任务，现行标准下9899万农村贫困人口全部脱贫，贫困县全部摘帽。中国在减贫方面取得的成果也为全球SDG1实现的进程作出了卓越贡献。

中国虽然解决了农村极端贫困问题，但农村发展仍面临诸多问题，如农业竞争力不强、城乡居民收入差距仍较大。对此，党的十九大提出了乡村振兴战略。

从发展角度来看，乡村振兴的提出重点是解决中国城乡发展不平衡，助力中国实现包容性增长。

由于历史原因，中国在过去实行城市与乡村二元结构的体制，这也导致农村经济长期落后于城市经济、农村居民生活水平落后于城市居民生活水平。近年来，中国城乡差距有不断缩小的趋势，2017—2021年城乡居民收入倍差由2.71缩小到2.5，但在教育、医疗等领域仍然有一定差距。鉴于城乡分离下的农村发展困境，中国在21世纪初提出新型城镇化发展战略，强调城乡统筹发展，在推动城乡经济和社会资源的统筹发展中发挥了巨大作用，但该战略是以行政推动实现农村人口向城市转移，是"改造乡村"并非"振兴乡村"[①]。因此，要解决城乡发展不平衡，重点是要激发乡村振兴的内生动力。

从政策角度来看，乡村振兴战略是"两个一百年"奋斗目标实现的必然要求。

党的十九大提出新时代中国特色社会主义发展的战略安排：第一个阶段，从2020年到2035年，在全面建成小康社会的基础上，再奋斗15年，基本实现社会主义现代化；第二个阶段，从2035年到本世纪中叶，在基本实现现代化的基础上，再奋斗15年，把我国建成富强民主文明和谐美丽的社会主义现代化强国。中国已宣布消除了绝对贫困，实现了第一个百年奋斗目标，但要实现建成社会主义现代化强国的战略目标，必然要求有与现代城镇生活匹配的、高度发达的乡村[②]，因此实施乡村振兴战略是实现第二个百年奋斗目标的必由之路。

从目标角度来看，乡村振兴在目标上更加多维，覆盖了经济、政治、文化、社会、生态文明等多个方面。

[①] 原超、黄天梁：《使乡村运转起来：乡村振兴战略的理论内核与行动框架》，《中共党史研究》2019年第2期，第15—23页。
[②] 张海鹏、郜亮亮、闫坤：《乡村振兴战略思想的理论渊源、主要创新和实现路径》，《中国农村经济》2018年第11期，第2—16页。

在时间线上，有两个重要时间节点，即2035年"取得决定性进展"，2050年实现"乡村全面振兴"。（见表2）

表2　乡村振兴的目标及时间线

2017年	党的十九大报告首次明确提出"实施乡村振兴战略"	总目标是"农业农村现代化"，总要求是"产业兴旺、生态宜居、乡风文明、治理有效、生活富裕"。
2018年	出台了有关实施乡村振兴战略的第一个五年规划《乡村振兴战略规划（2018—2022年）》	提出了乡村振兴的远景目标的时间线：到2035年，乡村振兴取得决定性进展，农业农村现代化基本实现；到2050年，乡村全面振兴，农业强、农村美、农民富全面实现。

（二）乡村振兴战略的五大支柱

考虑到乡村发展问题的复杂性，中国提出了系统化的解决方案，对应乡村振兴的要求，提出了五个实施路径。2018

图1　乡村振兴战略的五大支柱

年两会期间，习近平总书记提出"五个振兴"的科学论断，即乡村产业振兴、人才振兴、文化振兴、生态振兴、组织振兴，这五个方面是互相促进、不可分割的统一体。

1. 产业振兴是乡村振兴的基础和关键。产业兴旺是乡村振兴的核心和基础[1]。要实现乡村振兴，需要聚焦重点产业，挖掘资源要素，构建地域特色鲜明、业态模式多样、利益联结紧密的现代乡村产业体系、生产体系、经营体系[2]，提升乡村经济活力，带动农民增收致富。

2. 人才振兴为乡村振兴提供人力支撑。随着工业化和城镇化进程的快速推动，农村人口大量涌入城市，且以青壮年劳动力为主，农村人才不足已成为乡村振兴的突出短板。人才是引领发展的第一动力，是乡村产业、文化、生态、组织振兴的内生动力，迫切需要一批素质过关、能力卓越的强有力的人才队伍，为乡村经济社会发展注入"源头活水"。

3. 文化振兴为乡村振兴注入新的活力。文化是一个国家、一个民族的灵魂，在乡村振兴的过程中不仅需要注重中华传统文化的继承和发展，也需要充分利用乡村优秀传统文化的宝库，使其和产业有机融合并以此来支持乡村的长久

---

[1] 张海鹏、郜亮亮、闫坤：《乡村振兴战略思想的理论渊源、主要创新和实现路径》，《中国农村经济》2018年第11期，第2—16页。
[2] 汪晓文、李济民：《用系统观念理解和把握乡村"五大振兴"的辩证统一关系》，《社科纵横》2021年第5期，第46—51页。

发展。

4．生态振兴是乡村振兴的支撑点。一方面，中国积极应对全球的生态和气候危机，这要求农村和农业的发展走绿色低碳之路，以减少对生态环境的影响；另一方面，随着收入的增长，农村居民也开始对生活环境有了更高的要求，需要构建更加宜居的生活环境。

5．组织振兴是乡村振兴的根本保证。乡村振兴作为一项系统工程，不仅要提升各个参与主体自身的能力，也需要加强不同的组织和部门之间的配合。要建立健全党委领导、政府负责、社会协同、公众参与、法治保障的现代乡村社会治理体系[①]。

（三）乡村振兴的制度框架和政策体系

自乡村振兴战略提出以来，系列配套政策文件陆续出台，国家层面上乡村振兴战略的制度框架和政策体系逐步健全，工作机制也不断完善成型，为农业农村现代化建设打好了基础（见图2）。

---

① 汪晓文、李济民：《用系统观念理解和把握乡村"五大振兴"的辩证统一关系》，《社科纵横》2021年第5期，第46—51页。

资金支持	· 2020年中共中央办公厅、国务院办公厅印发《关于调整完善土地出让收入使用范围优先支持乡村振兴的意见》，对开拓乡村振兴资金筹措渠道、建立财政投入稳定增长的长效机制、提高土地出让收入用于农业农村的比例，作出了专门的制度安排。 · 2021年，中国人民银行和银保监会联合制定《金融机构服务乡村振兴考核评估办法》，以考核评估为指挥棒，督促引导更多金融资源配置到农村经济社会发展的重点领域和薄弱环节，对金融资源加大乡村振兴支持力度作出专门部署。
工作机制	· 国家层面推动实施乡村振兴战略领导责任制，实行中央统筹、省负总责、市县乡抓落实的工作机制，规定省级党委和政府主要负责人是本地区乡村振兴第一责任人。每年各省（自治区、直辖市）党委和政府向党中央国务院报告推进乡村振兴战略的进展情况。
法律保障	· 2019年和2021年国家分别出台了《中国共产党农村工作条例》和《中华人民共和国乡村振兴促进法》，把这些年关于脱贫攻坚和乡村振兴行之有效的政策体系、工作机制和工作方法等，以党内法规和法律形式固定下来。

图2　乡村振兴的制度框架和政策体系概况

（四）乡村振兴在中国发展战略中的重要意义

乡村振兴战略被写入了中国共产党章程，凸显了其对中国未来发展的重要性。乡村振兴战略和中国的其他政策优先事项相互补充、促进，其实施与实现共同富裕、构建"双循环"新发展格局、达成"双碳"目标和推进生态文明建设都有着密不可分的关系。

1. 乡村振兴是实现共同富裕的必由之路

乡村振兴和共同富裕的最终目标高度一致，都是不断满足人民群众对美好生活的需要。中国作为拥有近5亿农村常住人口的农业大国，必须依靠农村、农民实现共同富裕，乡村振兴在实现共同富裕过程中发挥着工具性作用和建构性作用①。

2. 乡村振兴是"双循环"新发展格局的坚实基础

中国面临着严峻复杂、挑战增多的发展形势，必须稳步提高风险抵御能力、发挥中国超大规模市场优势和内需潜力，形成以国内大循环为主体、国内国际双循环相互促进的新发展格局。实现该目标的重要路径，便是扩大最终消费和有效投资。中国农村是中国尚未充分开发的消费"蓝海"，如果通过乡村振兴有效提高乡村人均可支配收入，将极大促进国内大循环。

3. 乡村振兴是实现"双碳"目标和推进生态文明建设的重要抓手

农业中包含了有很强固碳功能的碳汇系统，故其对中国实现气候目标的作用不可忽视。同时，农村也是自然资源的富集地，是推进生态文明建设的重要阵地。因此，在乡村振兴的过程中，促进发展生态、绿色、低碳农业，能够同时助力多重目标的实现。

---

① 张琦、庄甲坤、李顺强、孔梅：《共同富裕目标下乡村振兴的科学内涵、内在关系与战略要点》，《西北大学学报（哲学社会科学版）》2022年第3期，第44—53页。

产业振兴篇

一、乡村产业振兴的内涵及意义

乡村产业既包括农村传统产业，也包括农村新产业新业态，还包括农村一二三产业的相互融合发展。产业振兴是乡村全面振兴的基础和关键，通过构建乡村产业体系，优化乡村就业结构，提高产业融合发展水平，实现乡村产业质量效益全面提升，拓宽农民增收渠道。特别是在当前我国经济面临下行压力，外部环境不稳定、不确定性凸显的情况下，需要将发展乡村产业放到更加突出的位置，增强乡村振兴的内生动力。

二、产业振兴的政策框架

自乡村振兴战略实施以来，有关产业振兴的政策体系和框架不断完善。2019年国务院印发的《关于促进乡村产业振兴的指导意见》对乡村产业概念作为了界定，并对乡村产业体系的重点内容进行了系统阐述。由此，推动乡村产业发展成为乡村振兴战略的一个重要内容。2020年农业农村部印发《全国乡村产业发展规划（2020—2025年）》，2021年农业农村部发布《关于拓展农业多种功能　促进乡村产业高质量发展的指导意见》，乡村产业发展政策不断健全，成为强农惠农政策的重要组成部分。

财政税收支持政策。党的十八大以来，国家强农惠农政策不断完善，对于"三农"的财政投入力度稳步加大。一方面，强化一般公共预算投入保障，加大对乡村产业发展的支持力度；另一方面，推动各地基金向乡村产业发展倾斜，要求提高土地出让收入用于农业农村的比例，支持乡村产业振兴。鼓励有条件的地方按市场化方式设立乡村产业发展基金，重点用于乡村产业技术创新。鼓励地方按规定对吸纳贫困家庭劳动力、农村残疾人就业的农业企业给予相关补贴，落实相关税收优惠政策。

乡村金融服务政策。党的十八大以来，历年中央一号文件都对强化金融服务乡村发展提出了要求和部署。国务院《关于促进乡村产业振兴的指导意见》也明确提出，引导县域金融机构将吸收的存款主要用于当地，重点支持乡村产业。支持小微企业融资优惠政策适用于乡村产业和农村创新创业。发挥全国农业信贷担保体系作用，鼓励地方通过实施担保费用补助、业务奖补等方式支持乡村产业贷款担保，拓宽担保物范围。允许权属清晰的农村承包土地经营权、农业设施、农机具等依法抵押贷款。加大乡村产业项目融资担保力度。支持地方政府发行一般债券用于支持乡村振兴领域的纯公益性项目建设。鼓励地方政府发行项目融资和收益自平衡的专项债券，支持符合条件、有一定收益的乡村公益性项目建设。规范地方政府举债融资行为，不得借乡村振兴之名违法违规变相举债。支持符合条件的农业企业上市融资。

社会资本参与政策。引入社会资本可有效减轻政府债务负担，缓解政府财政压力，同时也为企业带来直接和间接的收益。

国务院《关于促进乡村产业振兴的指导意见》明确提出，有序引导工商资本下乡。引导工商资本到乡村投资兴办农民参与度高、受益面广的乡村产业。支持企业到贫困地区和其他经济欠发达地区吸纳农民就业、开展职业培训和就业服务等。此后，农业农村部、国家乡村振兴局相继发布《社会资本投资农业农村指引》（以下简称《指引》）2020年、2021年和2022年。《指引》中提出了鼓励社会资本投资的13个重点产业和领域，并根据农业农村实际发展情况提出了全产业链开发模式、区域整体开发模式、政府和社会资本合作模式、设立乡村振兴投资基金、建立紧密合作的利益共赢机制等五种发展模式，为社会资本投入乡村发展和建设提供了指南。

用地保障政策。在安排土地利用年度计划时，加大对乡村产业发展用地的倾斜支持力度。推动制修订相关法律法规，完善配套制度，开展农村集体经营性建设用地入市改革，增加乡村产业用地供给。有序开展县域乡村闲置土地的综合整治，盘活建设用地[1]重点用于乡村新产业新业态和返乡入乡创新创业。

三、乡村产业振兴发展成就

中国全力推进乡村产业发展，夯实乡村振兴的物质基础，成效显著。

现代农业加快推进。坚持把保障国家粮食安全作为发展现代农业的首要任务，促进农业高质量发展。

2021年全国粮食总产达13657亿斤，连续7年保持在1.3万亿斤以上。

以建设高标准农田[2]为重点的农业基础设施条件明显改善，累计建成9亿亩以上高标准农田，实施国家黑土地保护工程。

新一代信息技术向农业生产、经营、管理、服务拓展。根据国家发改委数据，2021年，农业科技进步贡献率达到61%，农作物耕种收综合机械化率超过72%，分别比2017年提高3.5个、6个百分点。

---

① 建设用地，是指建造建筑物、构筑物的土地，包括城乡住宅和公共设施用地，工矿用地，能源、交通、水利、通信等基础设施用地，旅游用地，军事用地等。

② 高标准农田：系土地平整、集中连片、设施完善、农田配套、土壤肥沃、生态良好、抗灾能力强，与现代农业生产和经营方式相适应的旱涝保收、高产稳产，划定为永久基本农田的耕地。

乡村产业形态不断丰富。以乡村旅游业和服务业为代表的一批特色产业快速发展。2021年休闲农业和乡村旅游蓬勃发展，全国休闲农庄、观光农园、农家乐等数量达到30多万家，年营业收入超过7000亿元。全国农村网络零售额达到2.05万亿元，休闲农业和乡村旅游接待规模年均超过29亿人次。

乡村服务业创新发展，其中电子商务蓬勃发展，各类涉农电商超3万家，农村网络销售额突破1.3万亿元，其中农产品网络销售额达3000亿元。[①]

乡村产业融合也成为显著趋势。"农业+"文化、教育、旅游、康养、信息等产业快速发展。

利益联结机制不断完善。根据农业农村部数据显示，各地发展企农契约型合作模式，已有超过1亿农户与农业产业化龙头企业签订订单，签约农户总体经营收入超出未签约农户50%以上。推广利益分红型模式，通过"订单收购+分红""保底收益+按股分红""土地租金+务工工资+返利分红"等方式，促进农民持续增收。探索股份合作型模式，形成分工明确、优势互补、风险共担、利益共享的农业产业化联合体。[②]

---

① 《国家发展改革委举行新闻发布会介绍〈乡村振兴战略规划（2018—2022年）〉实施进展情况》，https://www.ndrc.gov.cn/xwdt/xwfb/202209/t20220928_1337507.html?state=123，2022-09-28。
② 韩长赋：《国务院关于乡村产业发展情况的报告——2019年4月21日在第十三届全国人民代表大会常务委员会第十次会议上》，http://www.npc.gov.cn/zgrdw/npc/xinwen/2019-04/21/content_2085626.htm，2019-04-27。

农村创新创业日渐活跃。建设近2200多个农村创新创业园区和孵化实训基地，累计有1120万人返乡入乡创新创业，平均每个经营主体带动6～7人稳定就业、15～20人灵活就业。

专栏1

推动水果产业绿色发展服务的脚步永不停歇
——贵州省开阳县南江乡醉美水果种植农民专业合作社

龙广村地处贵州省贵阳市开阳县南江乡，盛产枇杷。返乡村民陶秋运，利用枇杷果发展特色产业，不仅改变了自己的人生，更为龙广村"造"出了一条通往小康生活的"致富之路"。2014年，陶秋运回到老家牵头成立了开阳县南江乡醉美水果种植农民专业合作社，当时本地种植枇杷户均收入只有8000元左右。短短几年间，龙广村发生了翻天覆地的变化：从最初的几十亩果园，蝶变为拥有多个品种的上万亩果园。该村不仅注册了商标，还精心打造了无公害、可溯源的高品质水果品牌，通过互联网电商，远销全国各地。龙广村水果产业的蓬勃发展还带动了十里画廊乡村旅游业的发展。2021

年，龙广村户均收入显著提升，增至21000元。

搭建服务平台，聚焦全产业链服务

该合作社由龙广村11户农户自发组织成立，主要目的是促进当地枇杷产业的规模化和标准化发展。2016年发展社员43户，2017年发展社员113户。合作社作为服务平台，与产业、农户、专家紧密联系，在服务成员的同时也开展产品研发、拓展市场。合作社定期组织成员召开会议，商讨发展计划，针对在生产、销售过程中出现的问题进行研判处理。经过几年探索，合作社走出了一条"统一管理、统一技术、统一采购、统一用药、统一病虫害防控、统一价格、统一收购、统一品牌宣传、统一电商平台销售"的标准化作业路径。

重视产品品质，提升品牌附加值

合作社严控产品品质，在生产过程中，严格按照农产品安全监管要求，科学合理施肥及使用农药，定期采样送农业监管部门检测，要求合作社成员签订安全承诺书，做好内部监督，实现合作社产品可追溯，责任到人。此外，合作社注重区域品牌塑造，强化产品可溯源。目前，龙广村枇杷产业种植已实现前端和市场的对接，下一步，合作社还将把产业链延伸至深加工，进一步提高南江水果的产品品质和附加值。

种植类型增多，打通多元化销售渠道

合作社成立以来，枇杷种植规模已从最初各家分散种植、标准不一的状态，发展到如今已扩展到覆盖3个村庄的近万亩规模。为了破解"增产不增收"的农业产业发展瓶颈，合作社采取线上线下一体化销售模式。2021年对接北京、深圳、上海、昆明等城市水果批发市场及商超水果配送商，完成交易100多吨。此外，合作社还依托"十里画廊"丰富的旅游资源，组织开展现场采摘等活动。为促进自身健康发展，合作社在销售盈利中提取2%的利润作为滚动基金，用于产品包装开发、成员技术培训、营销开发等。

四、乡村产业振兴存在的问题

发展质量效益不高。乡村企业科技创新能力不强，特别是农产品加工创新能力不足，工艺水平落后于发达国家。产品供给仍以附加值较低的初加工品为主，休闲旅游普遍存在同质化现象，缺乏精准化、中高端产品和服务，品牌溢价有限。乡村产业聚集度较低，仅有28%的乡村产业集中在各类园区，规模效应有限。①但与此同时，部分地区和产业片面追求规模扩张和数量增长，导致无效供给增加、同质竞争加剧、质量效益下降的问题日益凸显。部分特色农业产业规模的扩张，还伴随着部分产品生产从适宜区向次适宜区甚至不适宜区的转移。这一趋势导致总体产品质量下降、品质分化加剧、竞争力弱化，甚至部分优质产品的生产发展遭遇劣质产品品质和声誉下降的拖累。

产业要素活力不足。乡村产业振兴稳定的资金、用地等要素投入机制仍不健全，对财政专项资金的依赖度过高，农村金融供给不足，选择性贷款现象严重，金融资源重城市、弱农村趋势更加凸显。农村资源变资产的渠道尚未完全打通，金融、社会资本进入乡村产业的意愿依然不强。

产业基础设施仍然薄弱。一些农村供水、供电、供气条件差，道路、网络通信、仓储物流等设施未实现全覆盖。产地批发市场、产销对接点、鲜活农产品直销网点的设施相对落后，物流经营成本高。

---

① 韩长赋：《国务院关于乡村产业发展情况的报告——2019年4月21日在第十三届全国人民代表大会常务委员会第十次会议上》，http://www.npc.gov.cn/zgrdw/npc/xinwen/2019-04/21/content_2085626.htm，2019-04-27。

人才振兴篇

一、乡村人才振兴的内涵及意义

实现乡村人才振兴有助于为乡村振兴战略的推进提供人力资本支持。长期以来，乡村中青年、优质人才持续外流，人才总量不足、结构失衡、素质偏低、老龄化严重等问题较为突出。数据显示：2021年，中国外出农民工数量达到17172万人，比上年增加213万人；平均年龄为36.8岁，大专及以上文化程度的占17.1%，农业转移人口多为年富力强、文化水平较高的青壮年劳动力[①]。在全面推进乡村振兴，加快农业农村现代化的背景下，乡村人才供求矛盾将更加凸显。因此，加快推进乡村人才振兴，充分发挥各类人才在乡村振兴中的引领作用，既是中央部署的工作要求，也是基层实践的迫切需要。不同于普通的乡村劳动者，乡村人才是具有一定专业知识或专门技能，在乡村工作或专门服务乡村，对乡村发展和农民增收做出贡献、起到示范带动作用的劳动群体。

2021年2月，为促进各类人才投身乡村建设，中共中央办公厅、国务院办公厅印发《关于加快推进乡村人才振兴的

---

① 国家统计局：《2021年农民工监测调查报告》，http://www.stats.gov.cn/xxgk/sjfb/zxfb2020/202204/t20220429_1830139.html，2024-04-29。

意见》，将乡村人才划分为农业生产经营人才、农村二三产业发展人才、乡村公共服务人才、乡村治理人才、农业农村科技人才（见图3），其中，农业生产经营人才与农村二三产业发展人才可以统称为乡村产业人才。

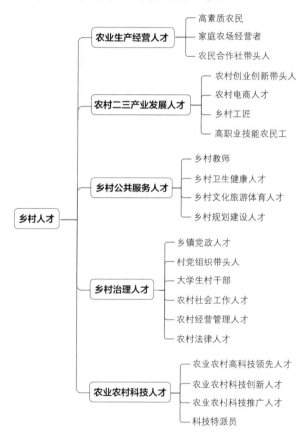

图3　乡村人才的类别

乡村产业人才。乡村产业兴旺离不开乡村产业人才。具体来看，高素质农民是破解"谁来种地"困境、确保粮食生产安全的核心主体；家庭农场经营者和农民合作社带头人是新型农业经营主体的重要组成部分；农村创业创新带头人、农村电商人才、乡村工匠、高职业技能农民工能够促进农村创新和经济持续活跃发展。

乡村公共服务人才。大力推进包括乡村教师、乡村卫生健康人才等在内的乡村公共服务人才的培养，是提升农村地区基本公共服务水平、促进城乡基本公共服务均等化的重要路径。

乡村治理人才。乡村治理人才是基层建设的"一线力量"。乡村治理人才包括两个大类：①乡镇党政人才、村党组织带头人、大学生村干部。他们肩负着贯彻落实"三农"各项方针政策的责任。②农村社会工作人才、农村经营管理人才和农村法律人才。他们作为不同领域的专业力量，在稳定农村社会关系、健全基层社会管理、助力公共法律服务下沉等方面发挥着重要作用。

农业农村科技人才。农业农村科技人才是推动农业科技创新和高质量发展的关键核心力量。其中，农业农村科技创新人才是指通过不断研发、引进和提供源头性的新技术，为乡村领域各项产业和事业发展提供前沿科技支撑的科技型人才；科技特派员是指经地方党委和政府按照一定程序选派，围绕解决"三农"问题，按照市场需求和农民实际需要，从事科技成果转化、优势特色产业开发、农业科技园区和产业化基地建设服务的专业技术人员。

二、推动乡村人才振兴的政策安排及成果

（一）乡村人才振兴的体制机制不断健全

1. 乡村人才培养制度

一是重视新型职业农民的培育。2017年《"十三五"全国新型职业农民培育发展规划》提出，要加快构建一支有文化、懂技术、善经营、会管理的新型职业农民队伍，支持涉农职业院校开展新型职业农民学历教育，并打造国家、省、县三级新型职业农民培育信息化平台。二是加快培育新型农业经营主体带头人。2017年《关于加快构建政策体系培育新型农业经营主体的意见》提出，要培育新型农业经营主体带头人，带动各地广泛开办新型农业经营主体带头人培训班。以山东省为例，其通过线上与线下相结合的灵活培训方式，为学员提供农业技能、经营管理等多方面指导。三是加强农村人才的实用技能培训。农业农村部启动实用人才带头人培训项目，开设农业农村电子商务专题培训班，各地也结合自身情况，统筹制定乡村人才素质提升和培养计划。例如，广东省积极开展技能培训项目，培养了包括厨师、家政服务人员以及技术工人在内的一批乡村人才。

2. 乡村人才引进机制

一是宏观政策上持续鼓励人才返乡创业。2015年，国务

院办公厅印发《关于支持农民工等人员返乡创业的意见》，鼓励农民工、大学生和退役士兵等人员返乡创业工作。此后，国家发展改革委会同有关部门组织开展返乡创业试点工作。2019年，人力资源和社会保障部等三部门联合印发《关于进一步推动返乡入乡创业工作的意见》，强化政策扶持力度。二是建立平台和载体以支持返乡人群，构建人才生态圈。2018年，多家机构联合发起"乡村振兴领头雁计划"，对返乡创业青年、农村基层干部、合作社及驻村企业负责人等新农人开展全面、系统的培训。2021年，农业农村部发布《全国农村创业园区（基地）目录（2021）》，向社会推介了2210家承载力强、功能全面、服务优质的农村创业园区（基地），吸引更多人员返乡入乡创业和人力资源。社会保障部建设创业孵化基地、返乡创业园等各类创业载体8800多家，为返乡入乡创业提供了低成本、全要素、便利化的孵化服务。

3. 城市人才定期服务乡村制度

一是开展多种项目促进优秀教育人才向农村基层流动。其中，"特岗计划"教师由教育部、财政部联合实施，通过公开招聘遴选高校毕业生到中西部的困难地区农村学校任教，服务期为3年，任教期间执行国家统一工资标准，由中央专项资金支付其工资性支出。2022年，其招聘规模达到6.7万名。

二是不断提升基层医疗卫生机构服务能力。国家开展了农村定向免费医学生培养、助理全科医生培训、县级医院骨干医师培训等项目，进一步充实了乡村卫生健康人才队伍。[①]2021年，支持中西部省份招收定向本科医学生6280人，培训助理全科医生6960人，为农村基层持续输送培养卫生人才；同时，启动了银龄医生进基层项目，充分开发退休医务人员人力资源，2021年共有529家机构，139名医务人员完成注册。

三是鼓励更多科技人才深入基层一线服务乡村振兴。科技部深入推行科技特派员制度，贯彻落实"三区"人才支持计划科技人员专项计划，2021年向全国22个中西部省区市和新疆生产建设兵团选派科技人员18072人，培训本土人员3534人。

（二）乡村人才振兴的政策保障更加完善

1. 乡村人才的资金投入保障

国家为返乡创业人员提供充分的补贴和优惠政策，包含一次性创业补贴、贷款贴息、贫困人员二次补贴等多种形式。2021年，中共中央办公厅、国务院办公厅印发《关于加快推进乡村人才振兴的意见》，要求落实乡镇工作补贴和

---

① 定向免费医学生培养，是指高考的特殊招生计划，在需签署合同承诺毕业后到基层医疗卫生机构服务6年的前提下，享受免除学费并获得生活补助的优惠待遇。

艰苦边远地区津贴政策，确保乡镇机关工作人员收入高于县直机关同职级人员。各地自主开展补贴工作，例如湖南省长沙市对认定为初级、中级和高级新型职业农民的，分别给予3000元、5000元和10000元的一次性补助。

2. 乡村人才的公共服务保障

2020年，农业农村部等9部门联合印发《关于深入实施农村创新创业带头人培育行动的意见》，要求加快推进全国统一的社会保险公共服务平台建设，切实为农村创新创业带头人及其所需人才妥善办理社保关系转移接续。2022年，农业农村部印发《"十四五"农业农村人才队伍建设发展规划》，鼓励各地打破乡村人才与城市人才在教育医疗、社会保障、公共服务等方面的政策壁垒，不断健全乡村人才的公共服务保障。

三、乡村人才振兴的主要经验

1. 立足农业、农村、农民的发展需求，有重点、有层次地推动乡村人才振兴

人才是乡村振兴的关键要素。近年来，中国采取一系列政策措施，不断补齐乡村人才短板，有效发挥了人才在乡村振兴中的支撑作用。一方面，通过对基础人才信息进行摸底采集和建档管理，加强了县乡村三级乡村人才管理网络建

设；另一方面，对标全面推进乡村振兴的目标任务和现实要求，重点排查乡村产业发展、公共服务提升、治理工作改善、科学技术进步等方面的人才瓶颈，通过细分乡村人才需求缺口，明确了人才培养的方向和目标。与此同时，在摸清乡村人才发展现状的基础上，中国根据乡村振兴需求制定人才发展规划，明确了乡村人才振兴的总体要求、重点任务、政策措施等，对各类人才进行分级分类培养，以满足不同阶段的急需紧缺人才需求。

2. 培育本土乡村人才和用好各类外来人才并重

为落实乡村人才振兴战略，中国坚持乡村本土人才培育和外来人才引进相结合的方式，加快乡村振兴人才队伍建设。在本土人才方面，充分利用乡村本土人才数量众多、乡情深厚的优势，通过开展本土大学生、退役军人、优秀青年农民以及务工返乡人员的培养工作，带动本土人才为家乡发展作出贡献；在外来人才方面，依托乡村振兴辅导员、专家服务团以及人才直通车等制度，引导城市人才积极服务乡村，根据外来人才的技能特点和兴趣爱好，合理分配其工作内容和服务地点，充分发挥外来人才的技术优势和服务热情。此外，中国推动建立县域专业人才统筹使用制度，利用"县聘乡用"和"乡聘村用"等方式，畅通城乡人才的流通渠道，在为各类人才提供更多选择机会的同时，赋予乡村基层更加灵活的用人自主权。

3. 不断完善乡村人才振兴保障机制

为推动乡村系统健康平稳运行，中国政府推动建立乡村人才振兴工作联席会议制度，把乡村人才振兴纳入人才工作目标责任制考核和乡村振兴实绩考核，不断加强农村工作干部队伍的培养、配备、管理、使用；通过加强乡村人才振兴投入保障、搭建乡村引才聚才平台、制定乡村人才专项规划、完善农村基础设施条件和公共服务水平等重要措施，推动"三农"工作人才队伍建设制度化、规范化、常态化。

文化振兴篇

一、文化振兴的内涵及意义

中国的传统和乡土文化是中国人民的"根"，是一种无形财富，善加利用不仅能够为乡村发展注入新的动力，而且能够提升农村居民在精神领域的福祉，也是实现乡村振兴总体目标里"乡风文明"的重要途径。文化振兴的主要内容包括以下两个方面：

一方面，在保护和继承传统文化的基础上，充分利用乡村的特有文化，发展相关文化产业和文化旅游业，以乡村文化资源的市场价值反哺乡村文化的发展。

另一方面，为农民提供高质量的文化服务，以满足其不断提升的精神文化需求。这要求乡村地区因地制宜建设现代化文化场馆，加强数字化技术应用，提高先进文化服务的可及性。除此之外，通过宣传活动，积极倡导现代科学文明并改善现存一些不良风气及传统，提高农民参与乡村治理的积极性和主动性。

二、文化振兴的重要举措

（一）制度保障

持续强化制度保障。从2015年起，中央连续设立支持地方公共文化服务体系建设补助资金，补助金额受各方面因素影响而有所波动。2021年中央支持地方公共文化服务体系建设补助资金共151.95亿元，与上年基本持平。该补助资金旨在引导和支持地方提供基本公共文化服务项目，改善基层公共文化体育设施条件，加强基层公共文化服务人才队伍建设等，支持加快构建现代公共文化服务体系，促进基本公共文化服务标准化、均等化，保障广大群众读书看报、观看电视、观赏电影、进行文化鉴赏、开展文化体育活动等基本文化权益。

在健全财政保障机制方面，2020年国务院办公厅发布《公共文化领域中央与地方财政事权和支出责任划分改革方案》，明确了公共文化设施免费开放作为中央与地方共同财政事权，以及中央财政应承担的基本补助标准和比例。除此之外，财政部会同有关部门建立了覆盖公共文化服务领域资金分配、预算执行、绩效评价全链条的管理流程，选取居民文化参与满意度等体现人民群众基本文化权益保障水平的绩效指标，对全国各地公共文化服务状况进行绩效评价，中央财政根据绩效评价结果安排地方奖励资金，通过正向激励的方式推动地方财政、文旅部门支持提供高质量的基本公共文化服务。

（二）推进农村移风易俗

2021年中央一号文件《中共中央 国务院关于全面推进乡村振兴加快农业农村现代化的意见》对"加强新时代农村精神文明建设"提出了更明确的要求。提出要持续推进农村移风易俗，主要目的是治理农村现存的一些不良风气及传统，如：高价彩礼、人情攀比、厚葬薄养、铺张浪费、封建迷信等。农业农村部于2020年、2021年先后开展两批全国村级"乡风文明建设"优秀典型案例推介工作，共公开推介了46个村级"文明乡风建设"典型案例。

（三）提升农村公共文化服务体系

2021年，文化和旅游部、国家发展和改革委员会、财政部联合印发《关于推动公共文化服务高质量发展的意见》，紧紧围绕公共文化服务发展中的重点领域和关键环节，提出了深入推进公共文化服务标准化建设、完善基层公共文化服务网络、创新拓展城乡公共文化空间、促进公共文化服务提质增效等九项具体工作。

在宏观计划层面，中国的"十四五"规划将"基本公共服务实现均等化，城乡区域发展差距和居民生活水平差距显著缩小"列为2035年基本实现社会主义现代化的远景目标之一。在此之后，文化和旅游部分别发布《"十四五"文化和旅游发展规划》和《"十四五"公共文化服务体系建设规划》，强调将推动城乡公共文化服务体系一体建设作为首要任务，着力补齐城乡基层短板，努力促进城乡协同发展，缩小城乡公共文化服务差距。

标准层面，国家发展和改革委员会、中央宣传部等部门联合发布《国家基本公共服务标准（2021年版）》，明确了目前阶段我国基本公共文化服务的主要范围，即公共文化设施免费开放、送戏曲下乡、收听广播、观看电视、观赏电影、读书看报、少数民族文化服务和残疾人文化体育服务等八个方面的内容，同时明确了各个项目的服务对象、服务内容、服务标准、支出责任和牵头单位，为各级政府履职尽责和人民群众享有相应权利提供了重要依据。

（四）保护和利用乡村优秀文化

在保护传承乡村文化方面，2021年中央一号文件提出要加强村庄风貌引导，保护传统村落、传统民居和历史文化名村名镇。加大农村地区文化遗产遗迹保护力度。从2012年开始，农业部持续开展中国重要农业文化遗产发掘工作。为了推动乡村特色文化产业发展，文化和旅游部发布《"十四五"文化产业发展规划》，提出要建设一批文化产业特色乡镇、文化产业特色村，促进乡村特色文化资源、传统工艺技艺与创意设计、现代科技、时代元素相结合。例如具有农耕特质的乡村文化产品、乡村休闲体验产品、农耕主题博物馆、村史馆、农耕手工艺、曲艺、民俗节庆等。

三、文化振兴发展成就

中国农村在文化传承保护、文化产业发展、文化素质提升等各领域都取得了较大进展，丰富充实了农村群众的精神文化生活。

（一）农村居民文化消费稳步增长

农村居民文化消费稳步增长。据国家统计局数据，2021年教育文化娱乐居民消费价格比上年增长1.9%，其中，城市居民教育文化娱乐消费价格同比上涨2.0%，农村居民教育文化娱乐消费价格同比上涨1.7%。2021年，农村居民人均教育、文化和娱乐支出1645元，较上年增长25.7%。

农村居民旅游消费快速增长。据《中华人民共和国2021年国民经济和社会发展统计公报》，2021年全年国内游客32.5亿人次，比上年增长12.8%。其中：城镇居民游客23.4亿人次，增长13.4%；农村居民游客9.0亿人次，增长11.1%。国内旅游收入29191亿元，增长31.0%。其中：城镇居民游客花费23644亿元，增长31.6%；农村居民游客花费5547亿元，增长28.4%。

（二）农村文化及体育基础设施建设得到优化

基层综合性文化服务中心建设取得积极进展，全国建成了村、社区综合性文化服务中心超过57万个，基本实现了全覆盖。全国约有94%的县（市、区）建成了文化馆的总分馆制，分馆数量3.2万个，93%的县（市、区）建成图书馆的总分馆制[①]，分馆数量4.9万个，城市书房、文化驿站、文化礼堂等一大批特色的文化空间遍布城乡社区。广播电视基础设施建设加强，农村广播节目综合人口覆盖率99.3%，农村电视节目综合人口覆盖率99.5%。根据中国互联网络信息中心数据，2021年农村互联网基础设施建设全面覆盖，现有行政村实现"村村通宽带"。截至2021年6月，农村网民规模为2.97亿，互联网普及率为59.2%，城乡互联网普及率进一步缩小至19.1个百分点。

全民健身"六个身边"工程遍及城乡，推动建立起覆盖面广、功能完善的全民健身公共服务体系，加快补齐农村体育场地设施建设短板，实现人人享有基本体育健身服务。《中华人民共和国2021年国民经济和社会发展统计公报》显示，

---

① 2016年12月26日，《文化部 新闻出版广电总局 体育总局 发展改革委 财政部关于印发〈关于推进县级文化馆图书馆总分馆制建设的指导意见〉的通知》印发，指出推进以县级文化馆、图书馆为中心的总分馆制建设，是构建现代公共文化服务体系的重要任务，对于有效整合公共文化资源、提高公共文化服务效能、促进优质资源向基层倾斜和延伸具有重要的推动作用。

2021年末全国共有体育场地397.1万个，体育场地面积34.1亿平方米，人均体育场地面积2.41平方米。基本建成覆盖全社会的全民健身组织网络，提升了农村基本公共体育服务水平。

（三）农村文体服务能力不断提升

基本公共文化服务标准化、均等化建设全面推进。2021年，中国农村电影公益放映发动全国268条院线5万余支放映队，在52.3万个放映点，全年放映800余万场，服务观众超6亿人次，丰富了广大人民群众的精神生活。

创新管理体制运行机制。政府向社会力量购买公共文化服务、统筹实施文化惠民工程等文化改革任务有效推进，在破除体制机制障碍、创新公共文化内容和方式等方面发挥了积极作用。

（四）乡村优秀传统文化有效传承

为了对具有历史、文学、艺术、科学价值的非物质文化遗产项目进行重点保护，2006年，国务院公布了第一批国家级非物质文化遗产名录（共计518项），截至2021年，已有五批共计1557个国家级非物质文化遗产代表性项目，其中有相当一部分项目为农村地区的传统文化、传统工艺，如京西太平鼓、秧歌等传统舞蹈，左权开花调、河曲民歌等传统民歌。

加强农业文化遗产保护利用。截至2021年，农业农村部已认定了6批138项中国重要农业文化遗产。经过六批发掘认定，中国重要农业文化遗产数量稳步增加，涉及的农业品类不断丰富、生态类型更加多样、区域和民族分布持续优化，尤其是中西部地区多项特色传统农业系统纳入保护范围，更为全面地展示了中国历史悠久、内涵丰富的优秀农耕文化。

持续推进传统村落保护工作。截至2021年，住房和城乡建设部已分五批将6819个有重要保护价值的村落列入了中国传统村落保护名录，建立了挂牌保护动态监管制度，在10个市州实施集中连片保护利用示范，建设了中国传统村落数字博物馆。村落单馆数量已达606个，覆盖全国31个省（区市）。通过持续努力，扭转了传统村落快速消失的局面，扩大了中华优秀传统文化的影响力。

专栏2

在乡村振兴战略提出之后，2018年中国首次在国家层面为农民设立节日——"中国农民丰收节"，由农业农村部会同有关部门组织实施。节日内容丰富多样，不仅包括为了促进农民增收而举办的线上线下农产品促销活动，也涵盖了一系列展示农耕文化的宣传活动，以提升大众对于农耕文化的理解和参与度。

生态振兴篇

一、生态振兴的内涵和意义

党的十八大以来，以习近平同志为核心的党中央以前所未有的力度抓生态文明建设，全党全国推动绿色发展的自觉性和主动性显著增强。2020年9月中国明确提出2030年"碳达峰"，2060年"碳中和"目标，绿色发展转型迈入新阶段。在全社会绿色转型的趋势下，生态振兴成为乡村振兴的应有之义，必须牢固树立和践行绿水青山就是金山银山的理念，推进乡村和生态的协调发展。在此大背景下，生态振兴的内容主要包含以下三个方面：

（一）农业绿色转型，实现生态与粮食安全双赢

促进农业生产的绿色低转型、碳转型，减少农业生产活动对于生态环境产生的负面压力。在全球气候变化的大背景下，农业既是温室气体排放源又是巨大碳汇系统，同时也是全球变暖、气候变化的受害者。气候变化引发的持续性高温、干旱、洪水等极端天气危及着农业的健康发展以及国家的粮食安全。因此要持续推进农业绿色发展，在有限的耕地、水资源条件下，用最小的资源环境代价生产出更多更优质的农产品，既保障国家粮食安全，也能催生农业新的增

长点和促进绿色消费。

（二）加快美丽乡村建设，提升农村人居环境

改善提升农民居住环境，满足农村居民对于良好居住环境的需求，加快美丽乡村建设。相比城市居民，我国农村人居环境总体质量水平不高，尤其在卫生设施、垃圾处理及污水处理方面还存在显著差距。因此，要以建设美丽宜居村庄为导向，以农村垃圾、污水治理和村容村貌提升为主攻方向，开展农村人居环境整治行动，全面提升农村人居环境质量。

（三）促进乡村生态系统保护与修复，筑牢生态文明基石

在生态文明建设的总体要求下积极促进乡村生态系统的保护与修复，自然生态系统功能和稳定性全面提升，使绿水青山持续发挥生态、经济、社会等多种效益。

二、农业生产加快绿色转型

聚焦重点领域和关键环节，持续推进农业用水总量控制、化肥、农药使用量减少，完成畜禽粪便、秸秆、地膜基本资源化利用的"一控两减三基本"的目标任务，以资源环

境承载力为基准的农业绿色生产制度逐渐形成，农业生产绿色转型取得显著成效。

（一）农业资源保护与节约利用不断加强

乡村振兴战略实施以来，中国在耕地资源保育、农业高效节水方面开展了大量工作，取得了积极进展，为农业绿色发展和生态文明建设提供了有力支撑。

1. 耕地资源保育卓有成效

2017年，原农业部印发《耕地质量保护与提升行动方案》，着力提高耕地内在质量，实现"藏粮于地"，夯实国家粮食安全基础。该方案明确了提升耕地质量、治理重金属污染以及解决"白色污染"等问题的具体目标。通过高标准农田建设、东北黑土地保护利用综合示范、土壤污染管控与修复、秸秆还田、有机肥替代化肥、轮作休耕、深松深耕和重金属污染防治等技术措施，实施耕地质量保护与提升行动，有效改善了耕地质量状况，2021年实施黑土耕地保护利用面积超过1亿亩。[①]通过以上一系列的耕地质量提升措施，全国耕地质量稳步提升，2019年全国耕地质量平均等级达到4.76等，较2014年提升了0.35个等级。

---

① 中国2016年正式颁布了《耕地质量等级》国家标准，全国耕地按质量等级由高到低依次划分为1至10等，农业农村部每5年开展一次全国耕地质量等级调查评价工作。

2. 农业水资源利用效率逐年提升

中国是一个水资源严重短缺的国家，水资源供需矛盾突出仍然是可持续发展的主要瓶颈。长期以来，中国高度重视农业节水，制定了最严格的水资源管理制度。2012年，国务院办公厅印发《国家农业节水纲要（2012—2020年）》，在文件的指导下，水利部与农业农村部联合推进农业水资源利用效率提升，在水资源紧缺、灌溉利用效率不高或水资源时空分布不均、供需矛盾突出的地区，因地制宜开展田间输水管道、喷灌、微灌等高效节水灌溉设施建设，增加有效灌溉面积，提高水资源利用效率和灌溉保证率，促进水资源集约节约利用。2021年，全国农田灌溉水有效利用系数达到0.568，较2011年前提高了0.052个点。

（二）农业面源污染防治成效显著

在《中共中央 国务院关于全面加强生态环境保护 坚决打好污染防治攻坚战的意见》《农业农村污染治理攻坚战行动方案（2021—2025年）》等强有力的政策推动下，农业面源污染治理实现了从治存量到遏增量的历史转变。

1. 化肥使用量持续减少

2015年，原农业部印发《到2020年化肥使用量零增长行动方案》，对提高化肥利用效率、促进增产增效和提质增效做出了具体安排。在文件的指导下，农业农村部持续推进化肥农药减施增效行动，2016年起全国化肥使用量连年下降，扭转了一直以来不断攀升的局面。2021年，全国农作物化肥使用量从2015年6022.6万吨（折纯）减少到5191万吨（折纯），减幅为13.8%（见图4）。

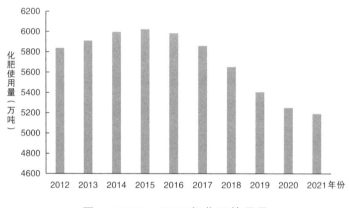

图4　2012—2021年化肥使用量

2. 农药使用量持续减少

2015年，原农业部印发《到2020年农药使用量零增长行动方案》，对提高农药利用效率做出了具体安排。在文件的指导下，农业农村部大力推进农药减量增效行动，实施绿色防控替代化学防治，及时准确预报病情虫情，推广高效植保药械，推行达标防治、对症用药、适时适量用药。病虫统防统治专业化服务组织蓬勃发展，减少个人施肥打药跑冒滴漏。截至2020年底，绿色防控面积近10亿亩，主要农作物病虫害绿色防控覆盖率41.5%、比2015年提高18.5个百分点，全国专业化统防统治服务组织达到9.3万个，三大粮食作物病虫害统防统治覆盖率达到41.9%，比2015年提高8.9个百分点。全国开展"百万农民科学安全用药培训"活动，指导农民和新型经营主体落实好减量关键技术，提升用药水平。随着科学施药理念日益深入人心，节药技术大面积推广，绿色高效产品加快应用，高效低风险农药占比超过90%。2021年全国水稻、小麦、玉米三大粮食作物农药利用率均超过40%，比2015年提高4个百分点。

3. 畜禽粪污资源化利用

农业生产过程中不可避免会产生农业废弃物，其中包括养殖业产生的畜禽粪便，以及农作物生长过程中产生的秸秆和农膜。这些农业废弃物如果处理不当，会对农村生态环境产生负面影响，因此加强农业废弃物资源化利用是发展循环经济、实现农业可持续发展的有效途径。2016年农业部联合其他五个部委发布了《关于推进农业废弃物资源化利用试点的方案》，旨在利用试点地区探索农业废弃物处理的有效技术路径以及综合利用模式。

2017年，国务院办公厅印发《关于加快推进畜禽养殖废弃物资源化利用的意见》，深入开展畜禽粪污资源化利用行动，加快推进畜牧业绿色发展。随后，原农业部印发《〈畜禽粪污资源化利用行动方案（2017—2020年）〉的通知》，对加快推进畜禽粪污资源化利用的重点任务进行部署，形成了以整县推进项目为重点，实施果菜茶有机肥替代、重金属残留检测等多方发力的政策体系。在文件的指导下，全国585个畜牧大县全部实施畜禽粪污资源化利用整县推进项目，2020年新启动实施120个非畜牧大县整县推进项目，提升畜禽粪污处理利用能力水平。2021年，畜禽粪污资源化利用取得积极成效，全国畜禽粪污综合利用率超过76%，比2015年提高了16个百分点，规模养殖场粪污处理设施装备配套率稳定在97%以上。

4. 秸秆综合利用

一方面积极推进农作物秸秆综合利用，有效解决秸秆出路问题，农业农村部以肥料化、燃料化、饲料化、原料化和基料化为主攻方向，在全国布局建设401个秸秆利用重点县。另一方面加强农作物秸秆禁烧管控工作。相关部门充分利用卫星遥感、无人机、高清摄像头等科技手段监测监控火点情况，开展秋收春播时节禁烧专项巡查，落实秸秆焚烧责任追究制度，秸秆露天焚烧现象大幅减少。2021年，全国农作物秸秆利用量6.47亿吨，综合利用率超过88%[①]，"五料化"综合利用格局基本形成。

5. 农膜减量与回收利用

农业农村部推动多部门协同治理"白色污染"，规范农膜生产者、销售者、使用者的行为，落实各主体回收废弃农

① 《〈全国农作物秸秆综合利用情况报告〉发布 2021年我国农作物秸秆综合利用率达88.1%》，http://www.moa.gov.cn/gbzwfwqjd/xxdt/202210/t20221010_6412962.htm，2022-10-10。

膜的法律责任，指导地方大力推广标准地膜，从源头提高地膜的可回收性，推动构建覆盖农膜生产、销售、使用、回收的全程监管体系。目前全国废旧农膜回收利用率超过80%，农田白色污染治理取得了重要进展。

（三）扎实推进农业生产"三品一标"①

2021年3月，适应深入推进农业绿色发展、提高农业质量效益和竞争力以及适应消费结构不断升级的需要，农业农村部办公厅关于印发《农业生产"三品一标"提升行动实施方案》的通知，提出从2021年开始，启动实施农业生产"三品一标"提升行动，更高层次、更深领域地推进农业绿色发展。

1. 加快推进品种培优

农业农村部实施打好种业翻身仗行动方案，加快选育一批新品种，提纯复壮一批地方特色品种，选育一批高产优质突破性品种，建设一批良种繁育基地。

2. 加快推进品质提升

农业农村部大力推广优质品种，推广集成技术模式，净化农业产地环境，推广绿色投入品，推广安全绿色兽药，构建农产品品质核心指标体系。

---

① "三品一标"是指品种培优、品质提升、品牌打造和标准化生产。

3. 加快推进农业品牌建设

农业农村部以培育知名品牌、加强品牌管理、建立农业品牌评价体系、强化农业品牌监管、促进品牌营销为重点，强化农业品牌建设。此外，还持续强化农产品质量监管，深入推进安全绿色优质农产品发展。

4. 加快推进标准化生产

农业农村部推动构建现代农业全产业链标准化建设，培育新型农业经营主体，健全社会化服务体系，助力农产品加工业升级，深化农产品精深加工，并在重点区域先行示范，以促进农业全面振兴。

截至2021年底，农业国家标准和行业标准超过1.3万项，基本覆盖主要农产品生产全过程。累计认证绿色、有机及地理标志农产品6.2万个，农产品质量安全监测总体合格率保持在97.6%以上，越来越多的绿色优质农产品端上了城乡居民餐桌。

三、农村人居环境持续改善

农村人居环境是实施乡村振兴战略和建设"美丽中国"的重要内容。实施乡村振兴战略以来，各地区各部门深入贯彻落实《农村人居环境整治提升五年行动方案（2021—2025年）》，认真学习浙江"千村示范、万村整治"工程经验，建立健全工作机制，扎实推进农村人居环境整治各项工作落实落地，开展美丽乡村建设工作，创建不同形式、各具特色的美丽乡村5万多个。

（一）农村生活垃圾治理全面覆盖

2019年，住房和城乡建设部指导各地落实《关于建立健全农村生活垃圾收集、转运和处置体系的指导意见》，加快推进收运处置体系建设。截至2021年底，全国农村生活垃圾进行收运处理的自然村比例稳定在90%以上，比2017年提高15个百分点。各地普遍采用"户分类、村收集、镇转运、县处理"的处理方式，部分条件较好的地区已推行城乡环卫一体化，95%以上的村庄开展了清洁行动，村容村貌明显改善。

（二）农村生活污水治理梯次推进

2019年，中央农办、农业农村部、生态环境部、住房和城乡建设部、水利部、科技部、国家发展和改革委员会、财政部、银保监会等九部门联合印发了《关于推进农村生活污水治理的指导意见》，指导各地结合农村实际，以污水减量化，分类就地处理，循环利用导向，走符合中国国情的路子。在文件的指导下，农业农村部、生态环境部等多部门联合推动农村生活污水排放标准和县域规划体系建立，120个县市区开展了农村生活污水治理示范，农村黑臭水体排查识别基本完成。截至2021年底，全国累计建成农村生活污水处理设施50余万套，全国农村生活污水治理率达28%左右。

（三）农村"厕所革命"扎实有效推进

2018年以来，累计改造农村户厕4000多万户，截至2021年底全国农村卫生厕所普及率超过70%。其中，东部地区、中西部城市近郊区等基础条件好的地区，实现无害化治理的农村卫生厕所普及率超过90%。

四、乡村生态系统建设取得明显进展

2012年以来，中国政府以前所未有的力度抓生态文明建设，并且提出统筹山水林田湖草沙系统治理的理念，一系列生态保护修复政策文件出台。《全国生态功能区划（修编版）》《全国生态保护与建设规划（2013—2020年）》《关于扩大新一轮退耕还林还草规模的通知》《全国草原保护建设利用"十三五"规划》《全国湿地保护"十三五"实施规划》等政策文件颁布实施，对于增强林业生态功能、保护草原生态、恢复湿地功能、生物多样性保护和恢复等起到积极作用，林地、草原、湿地、农田林网功能的恢复和提升将进一步促进乡村生态功能修复和提升。

（一）统筹推进山水林田湖草沙生态保护和修复，优化生态安全屏障体系

国家支持地方开展山水林田湖草沙生态保护修复，推动地方统筹自然生态各要素，实行整体保护、系统修复、综合治理，提升区域生态系统服务功能和生态环境质量。

1. 草原生态保护修复取得显著进展

在草原生态保护方面，不断加大对基本草原保护划定的监督检查力度，全面推进半农半牧区的基本草原划定工作，确立基本草原保护红线，重大生态工程区草原植被盖度比非工程区平均高出11个百分点，高度平均增加50%以上。同时，坚持基本草原保护制度，继续实施草原生态保护补助奖励政策和退牧还草工程，开展禁牧休牧、划区轮牧、舍饲圈养，推进草原改良和人工种草，促进草畜平衡，推动牧区草原畜牧业由传统的游牧向现代畜牧业转变。此外，退耕还林还草、退牧还草规模逐渐扩大，截至2020年底，草原综合植被盖度达到56.1%。

2. 基本建成农田防护林体系

中国积极推动实施重要生态系统保护和修复重大工程。截至2020年，全国农田防护林面积已达600多万公顷，主要农区已基本建成了集中连片的农田防护林体系。长江、珠江、沿海、太行山等防护林工程累计完成中央预算内投资

18.7亿元，安排工程建设任务513.92万亩，通过工程建设，工程区生态资源总量不断增长，林分质量持续提高，生态安全得到有效保障。

（二）积极推进水域资源保护，长江十年禁渔成效初显

2020年，农业农村部在长江流域重点水域全面实施"十年禁渔"，内陆七大重点流域禁渔期制度全覆盖，全国主要江河湖海休禁渔制度全覆盖。各地加快落实渔民安置保障工作，截至2020年底，中央财政安排补助资金130亿元并全部拨付到位，各地落实配套资金114.63亿元，累计落实社会保障21.8万人，帮助16.5万人实现转产就业。2021年，农业农村部印发《长江生物多样性保护实施方案（2021—2025年）》，以加强中华鲟、长江江豚、长江鲟等珍稀濒危物种资源保护为重点任务，统筹加强长江水生生物多样性保护。

组织振兴篇

一、乡村组织的基本内涵和意义

乡村组织振兴的对象是乡村组织，这些组织是指在乡村社会中为完成乡村政治、经济、社会、文化、生态等功能，按照一定形式和要求建立的乡村社会群体。按照组织设立的功能，目前中国乡村组织可分为政治组织、自治组织、经济组织和社会组织四大类型（见图5）。

乡村政治组织	乡村自治组织	乡村经济组织	乡村社会组织
• 包括在自然村、行政村设立的党小组、党支部、党总支，以及在其他农村经济组织、社会组织内部设立的党的组织。	• 包括村民委员会、村民会议、村民代表会议、村民监督委员会等。	• 包括农村集体经济组织、农村合作经济组织、农业企业、家庭农场、农业社会化服务组织等。	• 包括农村养老协会、妇女联合会、农村扶贫资金互助社、农村各类专业技术协会、新乡贤组织、红白理事会等。

图5　乡村组织类型图

1. 乡村政治组织

乡村政治组织主要指农村基层党组织。根据《中国共产党农村基层组织工作条例》，其负责"全面领导乡镇、村的各类组织和各项工作"，包括讨论和决定本区域内关于经济建设、政治建设、文化建设、社会建设、生态文明建设和党的建设以及乡村振兴中的重大问题。除此之外，村党组织也负责领导和推进村级民主选举、民主决策、民主管理、民主监督，推进农村基层协商，支持和保障村民依法开展自治活动。

2. 乡村自治组织

乡村自治组织是指农村居民实行自我管理、自我教育、自我服务、自我监督的基层群众性自治组织，是农民直接参与基层群众自治和民主活动的主要载体。

从20世纪80年代开始，中国在乡村实行村民自治制度。经过40多年的探索，形成了比较稳定的村民自治组织架构，包括村民委员会、村民会议、村民代表会议、村民监督委员会等。作为群众性的自治组织，村民自治组织和村民监督委员会是乡村的基本组织，是群众参与乡村治理的基本渠道和平台，具有广泛及时把握社情民意的优势，在促进乡村事业发展方面发挥着难以替代的重要作用。

3. 乡村经济组织

乡村经济组织是指为实现特定的经济目标而从事农业生产经营活动的组织形态。随着中国改革开放的全面推进和农村分工分业的日益深化，农村经济组织呈现出要素集聚、产销一体、产业融合和加速发展态势，家庭农场联盟、农民合作社联合社、产业化联合体、社会化服务联盟等新型组织模式不断涌现，合作制、股份合作制、合同订单等利益分享机制不断健全。

股份经济合作社，也可以称为经济合作社。中国实行农村集体所有制，土地为农村集体所有，由农民承包经营。农村集体经济组织是集体资产管理的主体，形成了特殊的经济组织形式。这种组织既常被称为经济合作社，同时也被称为股份经济合作社。

农民专业合作社是指在农村家庭承包经营基础上，由农产品的生产经营者或者农业生产经营服务的提供者、利用者共同组成的互助型经济组织。该组织致力于提供农产品的销售、加工、运输、贮藏以及与农业生产经营有关的技术、信息等服务，皆在通过自愿联合、民主管理等方式，实现成员间的互助与合作。它在发展乡村经济和提高农民应对市场风险方面作用突出。家庭农场由家庭成员担任主要劳动力，从事农业规模化、集约化、商品化的生产经营活动。家庭农场的特征表现为"家庭经营、规模适度、一业为主、集约生产"，其农业收入是家庭的主要收入来源。

农业企业是指从事种植业、畜牧业、林业、渔业和副业等生产经营活动的营利性经济组织，在整合农村土地资源、劳动力资源、资金资源、文化资源、技术资源、组织资源等方面具有自身优势。

4. 乡村社会组织

乡村社会组织是指在农村经济社会发展中发挥服务、沟通、协调等作用的非政府、非营利性组织，主要包括农村养老协会、妇女联合会、农村各类专业技术协会、新乡贤组织、红白理事会等。社会组织充分反映群众诉求、协调利益关系、提供专业服务。

不同的组织在乡村振兴各个领域都发挥着关键作用。例如：经济组织能够集结小农户以获得规模经济优势并抵御市场风险，有效助力产业发展。政治组织是人才振兴的关键，需要依靠其去引进人才、培养人才和凝聚人才。文化繁荣和生态振兴也离不开社会组织和自治组织，需要依靠其广大的民众基础，来鼓励更多村民参与到文化遗产保护、良好乡风建设以及保护生态环境的活动中去。乡村组织覆盖了乡村发展的各个方面，是落实乡村振兴的主体，因此需要通过完善相关支持政策、加强人才力量投入、加大资金支持倾斜等举措不断提升乡村组织的发展能力。

专栏3

乡村组织的特征

总体来看，乡村组织作为国家基层社会的管理组织，在历史发展沿革的过程中，具有其内在的统一性，其组织功能也随着乡村的发展演变而更加综合，组织成员的边界也因地域、生产活动等限制具有清晰的边界，组织结构也随着成员的相对固定而较为简单。

1. 组织功能的综合性

相比于城市组织的功能分化，长期以来乡村组织的功能是不分的。行政村一级的村党支部委员会和村民委员会①是一种功能交织、机构重叠的综合性基层组织，既是经济组织，也是政治组织，还发挥着社会组织的功能，呈现出政治、经济、社会"三合一"的综合性质。

2. 组织成员的固定性

城市的组织以及公司等组织，开放程度高，人员流动性比较大，而乡村组织的物质基础是土地集体所有，加之乡村开放性相对较低，其组织具有较为清晰的成员边界，组织成员较为固定。

3. 组织结构的简单性

由于乡村组织成员的身份比较单一，乡村的经济结构相对简单，农民的知识文化水平相对较低，乡村的人才等组织资源相对缺乏，乡村组织的治理结构往往比较简单。

---

① 村民委员会是村民自我管理、自我教育、自我服务的基层群众性自治组织，实行民主选举、民主决策、民主管理、民主监督。村民委员会办理本村的公共事务和公益事业，调解民间纠纷，协助维护社会治安，向人民政府反映村民的意见、要求和提出建议。村民委员会向村民会议、村民代表会议负责并报告工作。

二、乡村组织振兴的发展成就

（一）夯实自治组织基础，创新民主议事形式

改革开放以来，中国农村自治组织建设在全面推进中不断加强。首先，组织机构不断完善。中国农村基层自治组织已经逐渐形成决策权、执行权和监督权适度分离又相互制约的结构体系，形成了以村民会议和村民代表会议为主要决策机构、村民委员会为管理执行机构、村务监督委员会为监督机构的村民自治组织运行体系。其次，议事机制不断完善。全国开展多层次的基层协商，村规民约实现全覆盖，组织引导村民成立村民议事会、道德评议会、禁赌禁毒会等群众自治组织，高价彩礼、人情攀比、厚葬薄养等陈规陋习得到有效遏制。再次，法制建设不断完善。1998年颁布了《中华人民共和国村民委员会组织法》，2010年进行了修订。2002年、2004年、2009年、2018年中共中央办公厅、国务院办公厅分别就做好村民委员会换届选举、健全和完善村务公开和民主管理制度、加强和改进村民委员会选举下发了专门的制度文件。截至2021年，全国64万多个村（居）均配备了法律顾问。

专栏4

浙江秀洲：村规民约"约"出文明新风尚

为了使村民文明素养不断提升、村居发展更加和谐，近年来，浙江秀洲腾云村村委会坚持以群众为主体，编制符合民意的村规民约，探索基层治理新模式。

近年来，腾云村村委会在乡村振兴战略的不断推进下，完善村规民约内容，包括婚姻家庭、邻里关系、美丽家园、平安建设、民主参与、奖惩措施等方面，有效引导村民革除陈规陋习，培育文明乡风。在腾云村的村规民约中，美丽家园建设是其中之一，通过开展"门前三包"、垃圾源头分类等农村人居环境整治，致力"约"出乡村人居环境新风貌。同时，该村积极开展红马甲志愿服务，在村里进行卫生清洁活动，以实际行动引导村民参与村庄环境整治，形成共建共享治理新格局。

村规民约不是一纸空文，更不是墙上的装饰品，它是集广大干部群众智慧的成果，强化监督执行，才能让村规民约更有力度。腾云村每年开展先进评比，表彰奖励模范遵守村规民约的家庭和个人。凡违反村规民约的，对行为人酌情作出批评教育等相应处罚。

（二）壮大经济组织实力，发挥引领带动作用

中国积极探索壮大集体经济的有效途径，大力培育家庭农场、农民合作社、龙头企业、农业社会化服务组织等新型农业经营主体，中央一号文件多次提出要加快推动新型农业经营主体高质量发展，2022年农业农村部印发《关于实施新型农业经营主体提升行动的通知》，推动新型农业经营主体由数量增长向量质并举转变，为全面推进乡村振兴、加快农业农村现代化提供有力支撑。截至2021年底，全国共认定农业产业化龙头企业超过9万家，培育家庭农场390万个，农民合作社222万家。通过健全订单农业、利益分红、股权合作等利益联结机制，带着农民干、帮着农民赚，2021年农村居民人均可支配收入达到18931元，比2016年提升52.67%。

（三）培育发展社会组织，增强服务群众能力

党中央、国务院高度重视农村社会组织发展，2015年出台了《关于加强社会组织党的建设工作的意见（试行）》，2017年出台了《中共中央国务院关于加强和完善城乡社区治理的意见》，2020年出台《民政部关于大力培育发展社区社会组织的意见》政策文件，对农村社会组织的发展、管理、监督作了规范和完善。在国家政策的鼓励与支持下，农村的乡贤理事会、志愿者协会等社会组织逐渐兴起，在乡村治理

中发挥着重要作用。妇联组织作为国家治理体系的重要组成部分，在推进实施乡村振兴战略工作中，基层妇联组织积极发挥其示范引领作用，在农村产业发展、人居环境改善、乡风文明建设等方面，广泛动员广大妇女同胞，为实现乡村振兴贡献巾帼力量。除此之外，很多社会组织聚焦女性平等发展，积极开展相关项目，如中国乡村发展基金会与蚂蚁公益基金会联合发起的"数字木兰"项目，通过孵化县域数字产业与新型职业技能培训等方式，为处在中西部欠发达地区的女性提供多元化的就业机会和平台。

专栏5

河南内乡："巾帼"护水队守护一渠清水

清理垃圾、巡视河道、打捞水草、制止不文明行为……走进河南省内乡县岈曲镇彭营村，一群身穿红马甲的"女掌柜"志愿者正在丹江支流紫气河中忙碌着，火红的马甲和翠绿的水草交相辉映，成为一道亮丽的风景。

她们是由村内脱贫户和留守妇女自发组成的彭营村女子护水队。这样的志愿活动，她们每周都会抽出两天时间，投身于这些"有意义"的事情，致力于保护村内小溪及紫气河等水域，用实际行动守护一渠清水。"俺喊着村里姊妹们组建女子护水队，没事的时候清清河里的垃圾，一起守护家门口的'母亲河'，让村里吃上干净水。"女子护水队队长孙小英说，姊妹们一块有活干，有话聊，还能保生态。在孙小英的影响下，她24岁的女儿袁艳廷也加入了护水队。这支队伍也发展到十多人，她们在农忙之余参与护水志愿活动，保护水生态环境。

内乡县是南水北调中线水源地丹江口水库汇水区和主要水源涵养区，承担着一渠清水永续北送的政治责任。岈曲镇彭营村内的紫气河最终汇入丹江口水库。处于汇水区的岈曲镇，多年来一边整治生态环境，一边加速绿色转型，实现保水富民。

人居环境整治、留守群体服务、暑期安全提醒……不仅是护水，女子护水队在乡村综合治理中也发挥着重要作用，只要有需要，就有她们忙碌的身影。在女子护水队的努力下，紫气河的水更清了，环境更美了，村民的精神面貌也焕然一新。她们正为乡村振兴贡献着一己之力。

女子护水队主动担当、保护生态，保证了一渠清水永续北送，同时积极参与基层社会治理，为乡村振兴打下了坚实基础。该镇积极推进新时代文明实践活动，随着志愿服务意识不断增强，护水队引来了越来越多女同胞的加入，队伍也从一支变成了三支，陈家营村女子护水队和王井村志愿服务队，和彭营村女子护水队一样，她们从事志愿服务活动，弘扬正能量。

三、乡村组织振兴的经验启示

（一）坚持遵循乡村组织自身发展规律

专栏6

四川省米易县雷窝村：
红白理事会"理"出文明新风尚

雷窝村位于四川省米易县丙谷镇，全村面积20.44平方公里，下设14个村民小组，共有939户3425人。近年来，雷窝村为破解婚丧嫁娶大操大办、铺张浪费的难题，坚持以村党组织为引领，从村民自治出发，组建红白理事会，民主议定《村民公约》，打造红白事自办点，严格规范审批流程，理事会成员全程参与监督服务，党员干部带头示范，有效遏制了大操大办、盲目攀比等陈规陋习，减轻了"人情债"，刹住了"送礼风"，形成了勤俭节约、向上向善的文明新风尚。

一、组建理事会，选好"理事人"

2016年，在镇党委和村党组织的领导下，雷窝村采取自我推荐、组织推荐、群众推荐、村"两委"筛选评、挂村组干部审核评、村民代表集中测评"三荐三评"的方式，推选出了由村党总支书记任会长，6名甘于奉献、组织协调能力强、在村内有影响力并热心此项工作的党员和村干部任成员的雷窝村红白理事会。红白理事会在村党总支书记的领导下，全面参与村级红白事务，每月理事会对红白喜事的办理情况进行公布，广泛接受群众监督。对理事会成员工作不积极主动，引导群众喜事新办、丧事简办方面作用发挥不够，移风易俗政策宣传力度不足或者服务群众不到位的，由会长提议，经村"两委"审核、村民（村民代表）大会同意后，取消资格，并重新按照"三荐三评"的程序补充会员，选好"理事人"。

二、村民公约大家定

雷窝村红白理事会充分结合村级经济发展水平、民族习惯等实际，初步拟定村级红白事办理制度内容，在广泛听取村级乡贤能人、"两代表一委员"、挂村组干部、村民代表4个重要群体意见建议（即"四听"）的基础上，按照村党支部提议、村"两委"会商议、党员大会审议、村民（或村民代表）大会决议的"四议"程序，确定了以"卫生、健康、勤俭、节约"八个字为核心、"宴席不超30桌，菜品只有9大碗，送礼不过200元"为标准的《雷窝村红白喜事村民公约》。

三、全流程参与监督服务

在红白事操办过程中，理事会人员全程参与，就宴席饮食卫生和规模，以及是否借机敛财、是否大操大办、是否铺张浪费等进行现场查看并提取菜品留样监测，对红白事操办人提出意见建议，在有效保障食品安全的同时扎实推进移风易俗。在红白喜事自办点办理宴席，统一了办理标准，村民节省了成本，村集体盘活了闲置资产，实现村民、村集体双赢。目前全村"人情"负担减轻70%以上。如今，红白事先申报，后到"自办点"操办，重"里子"轻"面子"，已经成为全体雷窝村民的共同认识和自觉行动。

实现乡村组织振兴要顺应组织自身发展规律，在组织建设过程中尊重乡村发展的客观现实，兼顾不同区域、不同发展阶段的乡村组织发展现状，因地制宜、分类指导，确保乡村组织建设经得起历史和群众检验。实践过程中，全国各地区在农村基层党组织领导下，因地制宜、因需施策，依据当地特点有序有效推进乡村组织振兴，成立了农村集体经济组织、农民专业合作组织、农村社会组织等各种类型乡村组织，取得了一定实效。实践证明，实现乡村组织振兴，需要充分尊重乡村组织发展的客观规律，科学把握乡村组织的差异性和发展走势分化特征，以解决实际问题为着眼点，综合考量当地资源禀赋和各种场景下政府、市场、农民等多方主体的各类需求，坚持党建引领、各司其职、分步实施、科学推进。

（二）坚持正确处理好乡村组织之间的边界

专栏7

张家港永联村的改革实践：村庄里的大气象

永联村位于江苏省苏州张家港市，近年来，伴随着工业化、城镇化的发展，为适应新情况、解决新问题，永联村探索形成了与时俱进的乡村治理模式，实现了由穷村变富村、小村变大村、传统乡村发展成为现代化农村的华丽转身。

　　第一，由村企合一向村企合伙、村企合作转变。永联村成立村经济合作社来维护农民的经济利益。永联村的经济合作社是在农村双层经营体制下，由永联村集体经济组织成员以集体土地、集体资产、集体资本为纽带组成的经济联合体，坚持集体所有、合作经营、民主管理、成果共享的原则，承担集体资源的开发与利用、资产的经营和管理、生产发展与服务、财务管理与分配等职责，实行自主经营、独立核算。

　　第二，由小村庄办社会向公共管理、公共服务均等化转变。永联村成立镇社会管理服务中心永联分中心。南丰镇政府和永联村多次磋商、实践与探索，最终确定成立镇社会管理中心永联分中心。该中心建立了一个综治平台——永联村事务管理服务协调小组，该小组由公安、交通、城管、卫生、工商、消防等执法机构和人员组成，承接乡镇政府延伸至村内的公共管理和公共服务，乡镇政府与永联村组织合作，确保永联村公共秩序得到稳定，公共管理和公共服务均等化。

　　第三，打造乡村共同体。永联村在文明乡风建设时联合五大治理主体，共同打造社区文化空间，推广社区文化活动。目前，永联小镇范围内已经形成了联合共建的主体框架，社会组织等在文化空间的改造以及文化活动的推广中贡献了巨大的力量。

江苏省张家港市永联村充分发挥村民自治民主机制，理顺村企关系，进行股份制改造，走向现代企业自我运行的路子。同时，在党组织领导下，永联村乡村治理体系更加完善，各个治理主体职责清晰，分工明确。2020年，永联村成功入选全国乡村治理示范村。

乡村组织类型多样，党组织、自治组织、市场组织与社会组织的功能作用各有侧重。实现乡村组织振兴，既要强化农村基层党组织的领导责任，也要充分发挥自治组织在农村社会事务管理中的核心作用，同时要充分发挥市场组织在资源配置中的决定性作用，更要发挥社会组织在政府和市场失灵领域的重要作用，实现党组织、自治组织、市场组织与社会组织协同互动的良好局面。

实践证明，推进乡村组织振兴，党组织、自治组织、市场组织与社会组织互为补充、缺一不可，必须在党组织领导下，把村民委员会的自治功能发挥好，同时为发挥市场组织作用创造有利条件，推动生产要素在农业农村领域优化配置，有效推动社会组织蓬勃兴起，推动社会进步，切实形成推动乡村组织振兴的强大合力。

翻转进入中文版阅读

RURAL REVITALIZATION IN CHINA

(International Edition)

EDITED BY RCRE

中国出版集团有限公司
研究出版社

Disclaimer

The designations and the presentation of the materials used in this publication do not imply the expression of any opinion whatsoever on the part of the United Nations concerning the legal status of any country, territory, city or area or of its authorities, or concerning the delimitation of its frontiers or boundaries. The views expressed in this publication are those of the author(s) and do not necessarily reflect the views or policies of the United Nations (UN) and the United Nations Development Programme (UNDP). The research team has made its best efforts to ensure the accuracy of the data and information included in this publication, but does not guarantee that the information and suggestions will be free from change and assumes no liability or responsibility for any consequence of their use. The analysis included in the report was finalized by October 2022.

Executive summary

This report summarizes **China's actions and achievements** in enhancing living standards as well as agricultural output in the countryside, through **its rural revitalization strategy**. It also highlights key policy documents supporting this, including the Strategic Plan for Rural Revitalization Strategy (2018—2022); its **phased goals for rural revitalization; and the 'five pillars' guiding this**.

By implementing its rural revitalization strategy and other relevant national strategies, including the poverty alleviation campaign, rural areas of China are catching up with the rapid pace of urban development. These positive developments and results provide valuable insights, best practices and lessons learned on pragmatic approaches to advance rural development across various provinces in China.

A notable approach in China's rural revitalization strategy has been its emphasis on **enhancing the role of technology in the agricultural**

sector to increase agricultural outputs and contribute to food security. According to the National Development and Reform Commission (NDRC) in 2022[1], more than 72 percent of ploughing, planting and harvesting was mechanized, up 6 percentage points from 2017. This has helped to lift China's per capita grain output, reaching 483 kg in 2021, compared with 472 kg in 2018[2].

In tandem with agricultural development, the report also highlights how **rural incomes have grown**, consolidating decades of dedicated efforts in addressing poverty alleviation, with the government announcing its achievement in meeting its goal of eradicating extremely rural poverty by the end of 2020[3]. Rural residential incomes continued to climb, with the urban-rural income gap falling to 2.5:1 in 2021[4].

The rural revitalization strategy has also focused on ensuring a more livable environment in rural areas. Since 2018, more

---

[1] News Center of the State Council of the People's Republic of China, 29 Sep,2022, *Continue to steadily promote the comprehensive revitalization of rural areas -- The relevant heads of the two departments talk about the progress of the implementation of the strategic plan for rural revitalization*. Retrieved from: https://www.gov.cn/ xinwen/2022-09/29/content_5713520.htm

[2] News Center of the State Council of the People's Republic of China, 14 Sep 2023, *Major indicators such as grain output, per capita grain occupancy, and grain sown area have all increased -five sets of data to see the stability of "China's rice bowl."* Retrieved from: https://www.gov.cn/ yaowen/liebiao/202309/content_6903859.htm

[3] The State Council Information Office of the People's Republic of China, (2021), *Poverty Alleviation: China's Experience and Contribution*. Retrieved from: https://language. chinadaily.com. cn/a/202104/06/WS606bffe7a31024ad0bab3c43.html

[4] News Center of the State Council of the People's Republic of China, 11 Oct 2022, *National Bureau of Statistics: The relative income gap between urban and rural residents has continued to narrow in the past 10 years*. Retrieved from: https://www.gov.cn/xinwen/2022-10/11/content 5717714.htm

than 40 million rural household toilets around the country have been renovated, with more than **70 percent of rural households now having access to sanitary toilets**[①]. The system for collecting, transferring, treating and disposing of domestic waste now also covers more than 90 percent of villages[②].

China's rural revitalization strategy also emphasizes the importance of protecting arable land, **water- saving irrigation,** as well as agricultural resource conservation and utilization. The average quality rating of China's arable lands has improved from 5.11 in 2014, to 4.76 in 2019[③]. By the end of 2019, 226,000 square kilometers of land in China was upgraded with water-saving irrigation[④]. The use of **chemical fertilizers and pesticides has also fallen** prominently during the 13th Five-Year-Plan (2015—2020)[⑤].

Despite these achievements, a key challenge identified is rural to urban migration, resulting in the **steady outflow of talented**

[①] News Center of the State Council of the People's Republic of China, 28 Jun 2022, *More than 70 percent of rural residents have access to sanitary toilets*. Retrieved from: https://www.gov.cn/xinwen/2022-06/28/content_5698070.htm

[②] ibid

[③] According to the national standard on "quality of arable land rating" (2016), the quality is rated from 1-10, with 1 being the best quality land.

[④] News Center, Ministry of Agriculture and Rural Affairs of the People's Republic of China, 13, Jul 2021, *Agricultural modernization brilliant five-year series of publications No. 23: Vigorously promote agricultural water-saving to ensure national food security*. Retrieved from: http://www.jhs.moa.gov.cn/ghgl/202107/t20210713_6371688.htm

[⑤] News Center, Ministry of Agriculture and Rural Affairs of the People's Republic of China, 16, Jul 2021, *Agricultural modernization brilliant five-year series of publications XXVI: zero growth of fertilizer and pesticide use has achieved significant results*. Retrieved from: http://www.ghs.moa.gov.cn/ghgl/202107/t20210716_6372084.htm

and educated individuals who largely continue to move from the countryside to cities. To effectively retain and attract human capitals for rural development, a **series of policies and measures to progressively expand its rural human resource pool have been undertaken,** including providing targeted education and training opportunities, creating incentives for talented individuals to remain in or return to rural areas, as well as fostering rural entrepreneurship and innovation. Lessons learned have indicated that such efforts must continue to be expanded further in the future, to ensure their lasting effectiveness.

Overall, China's experience in rural revitalization offers valuable insights and lessons for global learning on accelerating progress towards the *2030 Agenda for Sustainable Development* and the 17 Sustainable Development Goals (SDGs), [1] to end poverty everywhere and protect the planet.

The actions and achievements from China's rural revitalization strategy also underscore the critical importance of all stakeholders playing their part in achieving the SDGs. This encompasses the need for a whole-of-government approach in forming and implementing policies; unlocking the positive role of the private sector to accelerate inclusive socio-economic growth; leveraging technical insights and development solutions from academia; as well as engaging local communities in co-designing and

---

① The 2030 Agenda for Sustainable Development and the 17 Sustainable Development Goals was adopted unanimously by all United Nations Member States in 2015 and serves as the blueprint for global and national development. The full text is available at: https://sdgs.un.org/2030agenda

implementing solutions for an inclusive, sustainable and resilient future.

October 2020, Agricultural technicians in Baying County, Aksu Prefecture, Xinjiang Uyghur Autonomous Region, explain vegetable planting techniques to the masses.

Source of pictures:National Publicity and Education Center for Rural Revitalization

Contents

Organizational Revitalization

Introduction

Source of pictures:National Publicity and Education Center for Rural Revitalization

Background

In 2017, to boost rural development and narrow the longstanding urban-rural income gap, China proposed a rural revitalization strategy based on a range of policy interventions at multiple levels. The strategy is now more relevant than ever, following the devasting impact of COVID-19, which reversed development gains for the first time in three decades. According to *the Human Development Report 2021/2022*, the global Human Development Index (HDI) value declined for two consecutive years for the first time since it was established in 1990, back to the level of 2016. This report provides an account of China's actions and experiences in rural revitalization, while introducing its policies and achievements in promoting rural development.

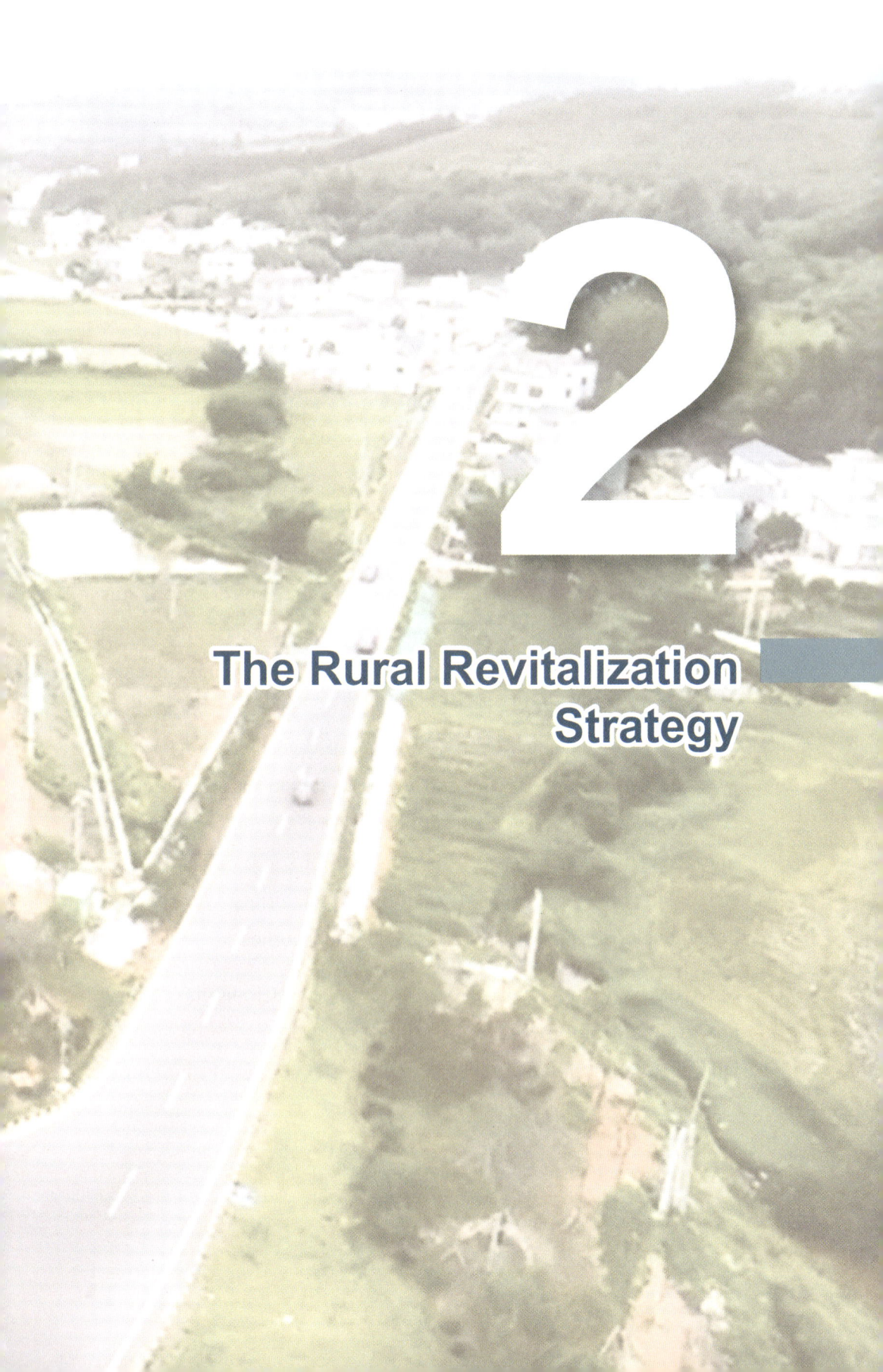

2

The Rural Revitalization Strategy

2.1 The Emergence of the Rural Revitalization Strategy

With a population of 1.4 billion, China is the world's largest developing economy, having confronted severe poverty challenges. Since its opening-up and reform, China has reduced the number of people living in poverty by over 770 million. [1]In doing so, it has made a significant contribution to the global fight to end poverty. Over the last decade, the Chinese government has enhanced efforts in devising a targeted rural poverty alleviation strategy, involving significant investments in human and financial resources. This required precisely identifying rural poor household and the causes of their poverty, followed by a package of targeted assistance measures. By the end of 2020, China had achieved its poverty alleviation target – to eradicate rural extreme poverty, as planned. However, despite this remarkable success, challenges remain in rural development, including agricultural weaknesses, underdeveloped rural infrastructure and low incomes.

Since the beginning of the People's Republic of China, the country has gradually adopted a dual urban- rural economic structure, leading to some longstanding economic development challenges

---

[1] Maria Ana Lugo, Martin Raiser & Ruslan Yemtsov, *What's next for poverty reduction policies in China?* World Bank Blogs, Oct 15, 2021. Retrieved from: https://blogs. worldbank.org/ eastasiapacific/whats-next-poverty-reduction-policies-china

and lower living standards in rural areas. [1]In an early attempt to address the problems of rural development under this dual economic structure, China proposed a new urbanization strategy with a focus on coordinated development for both urban and rural areas. While this helped to boost urban-rural economic growth and coordinate social resources, it also adopted administrative measures to encourage the migration of rural residents to urban areas, not necessarily promoting their revitalization. The dilemma of China's rural governance was therefore not resolved during the country's recent institutional changes and social transformation.

It became evident that to balance urban and rural development, it was essential to stimulate the intrinsic drivers of socio-economic development in rural areas. Recent years have witnessed a narrowing of the gap between urban and rural development, with the urban-rural income gap shrinking from 2.71 in 2017, to 2.5 in 2021[2]. However, inequalities remain in areas like education and healthcare.

To address these challenges, the 19th National Congress of the CPC, held in 2017, proposed a rural revitalization strategy under

[1] The urban-rural dual economic structure originated in the era of the planned economy. Different models were adopted in urban and rural governance, as well as economic development. One manifestation, which is caused by the household registration system, is the gap in welfare provision between rural and urban households.

[2] Press Release Center of the State Council Information Office of the People's Republic of China, Sep 28th 2022, *The National Development and Reform Commission held a press conference on the progress of the implementation of the Rural Revitalization Strategic Plan (2018—2022)*, Retrieved from: http://www.scio.gov.cn/xwfb/bwxwfb/gbwfbh/ fzggw/202211/t20221111_618756.html

Local government workers in Jiaoqu County, Linfen City, Shanxi Province, introduce the "One Code" method to impoverished residents, bridging the information gap for local people.

Source of pictures: National Publicity and Education Center for Rural Revitalization

the broader framework of the "Two Centenary Goals ." [1]Realizing a fully developed countryside with a standard of living comparable to modern urban life [2]is an essential part of achieving China's Second Centenary Goal.

Rural revitalization is the continuation, extension and upgrade of the poverty alleviation strategy. It has a broader range of objectives, covering the economy, politics, culture, environmental and social issues. The ultimate aim is to realize "modernization in agriculture and rural areas", through "thriving businesses, a pleasant living environment, a cultured and civil social environment, effective

---

[1] The CPC drew up a development plan for the new era at its 19th National Congress. In the first stage, from 2020 to 2035, we will build on the foundation of the moderately prosperous society with 15 more years of hard work to see that socialist modernization is basically achieved. In the second stage, from 2035 to the middle of the 21st century, having achieved basic modernization, we will work hard for 15 more years and develop China into a great modern socialist country that is prosperous, strong, democratic, culturally advanced, harmonious, and beautiful.

[2] Haipeng, Z., Liangliang, G., & Kun, Y. (2018). Strategic Thinking on Rural Revitalization Strategy: Theoretical Origin, Main Innovation and Realization Path. *Chinese Rural Economy* (11), 2-16.

governance and prosperity." [1]Two critical milestones have been set: to achieve "pivotal progress" by 2035 through basic modernization of agriculture and rural areas, as well as realizing all-round rural revitalization by 2050.

2.2 Five Pillars of Rural Revitalization

Taking into account the complexity of rural contexts and development, a holistic approach consisting of five pillars of rural revitalization was proposed by President Xi Jinping during the National People's Congress and the Chinese People's Political Consultative Conference (the "two sessions") in 2018, after which the *Strategic Plan for Rural Revitalization (2018—2022)* was issued by the Central Committee of the CPC and the State Council. The five pillars aim to promote "industrial, human capital, cultural, environmental and organizational revitalization" in rural areas (Figure 1).

---

[1] Jinping X. (2017). *The 19th National Congress report.* Beijing, China: People's Publishing House

Figure 1: Five Pillars of Rural Revitalization

Source: Authors

The key elements are outlined as follows:

a) Industrial revitalization is the foundation of rural revitalization. To revitalize rural areas, it is essential to generate economic opportunities, as well as promote job and income generation. The focus is on promoting targeted sectors and tapping available resources to build a modern rural industrial system, by leveraging unique local characteristics and diversified business models[1].

---

[1] Xiaowen, W., & Jimin, L. (2021). Understanding the Dialectical Relationship Among Five Revitalizations of Rural Revitalization from a Systematic Perspective *Social Sciences Review*, 36(05), 46-51.

b) Human capital revitalization provides human support for rural revitalization.

A skilled and qualified workforce is urgently needed, to empower rural social and economic growth, while also driving industrial, cultural, environmental and organizational revitalization in rural areas.

c) Cultural revitalization injects new vitality into rural revitalization.

In the process of rural revitalization, cultural traditions should be safeguarded and developed, taking full advantage of China's rich historic rural culture, which can be used as an asset in industries targeting sustainable rural development.

d) Ecological revitalization serves as the supporting point for rural revitalization.

Rural revitalization entails green and low-carbon development of rural areas and the agricultural sector to mitigate environmental harm. Alongside demand for higher incomes, rural residents are also demanding a more livable environment.

e) Organizational revitalization is the fundamental guarantee of rural revitalization.

Rural revitalization depends not only on capable individual participants, but also on enhanced collaboration among organizations and departments. It also calls for a modern social governance system led by Party committees and implemented by local authorities, based on consultation, coordination, broad

participation, along with rule of law[1].

To effectively evaluate the implementation and progress of the rural revitalization initiatives, the *Strategic Plan for Rural Revitalization (2018—2022)* identified 22 indicators (see Table 1). These are designed according to the five objectives: thriving businesses, a pleasant living environment, a cultured and civil social environment, effective governance and prosperity.

A mapping between these indicators and its focus areas against the key dimensions/ objectives of the global indicators of the SDGs [2] shows congruence of a number of priorities in areas such as eradicating poverty, ensuring food security, ensuring basic public services, narrowing the gap between urban and rural areas, along with promoting green and sustainable development (Table 1).

---

[1] Qi, Z., Jiakun, Z., Shunqiang, L., & Mei, K. (2022). Scientific Connotation, Inner Relationship and Strategic Key Points of Rural Revitalization under the Goal of Common Prosperity. *Journal of Northwest University (Philosophy and Social Sciences Edition), 52(03), 44-53.*

[2] The global indicator framework includes 231 unique indicators. Please note that the total number of indicators listed in the global indicator framework of SDG indicators is 248. However, thirteen indicators repeat under two or three different targets.

Table 1[1] : Correspondence between Major Rural Revitalization Indicators[2] and Focus Areas of the SDGs

	Major Rural Revitalization Indicators		Corresponding SDGs with similar objectives/ focus dimensions
1	Combined grain production capacity	SDG 2	End hunger, achieve food security and improved nutrition and promote sustainable agriculture
2	Cont r ib ution rate of scientific a nd technological progress in agriculture	SDG 2	End hunger, achieve food security and improved nutrition and promote sustainable agriculture
3	Agricultural labor productivity	SDG 2	End hunger, achieve food security and improved nutrition and promote sustainable agriculture
4	The ratio of processed agricultural product output value to the total agricultural output value	SDG 2	End hunger, achieve food security and improved nutrition and promote sustainable agriculture
5	Leisure agriculture and agritourism person- times	SDG 8	Promote sustained, inclusive and sustainable economic growth, full and productive employment and decent work for all
6	Overall utilization rate of livestock and poultry manure	SDG 12	Ensure sustainable consumption and production patterns
7	Greenery coverage rate in villages	SDG 15	Protect, restore and promote sustainable use of terrestrial ecosystems, sustainably manage forests, combat desertification and halt and reverse land degradation and halt biodiversity loss
8	Ratio of villages that implement household waste management	SDG 6	Ensure availability and sustainable management of water and sanitation for all

① The table is based on the author's analysis.
② Policy Documents of the State Council of the People's Republic of China 26, Sep 2018, *CPC Central Committee and State Council issues Strategic Plan for Rural Revitalization (2018—2022)*. Retrieved from: https://www.gov.cn/zhengce/2018-09/26/content_5325534.htm

Continued Table

Major Rural Revitalization Indicators		Corresponding SDGs with similar objectives/ focus dimensions	
9	Penetration rate of sanitary facilities in rural areas	SDG 6	Ensure availability and sustainable management of water and sanitation for all
10	Coverage rate of village comprehensive culture service centers①	SDG 8	Promote sustained, inclusive and sustainable economic growth, full and productive employment and decent work for all
11	Ratio of county-level and above villages and towns that received the honor of "civilized villages and towns"②	SDG 8	Promote sustained, inclusive and sustainable economic growth, full and productive employment and decent work for all
12	Proportion of full-time teachers in rural compulsory education schools with a bachelor's degree or above	SDG 4	Ensure inclusive and equitable quality education and promote lifelong learning opportunities for all
13	Proportion of rural resident's spending on education, cultural activities and entertainment	SDG 4	Ensure inclusive and equitable quality education and promote lifelong learning opportunities for all
14	Coverage rate of village planning and management③	SDG 11	Make cities and human settlements inclusive, safe, resilient and sustainable
15	Proportion of villages with integrated service stations④	SDG 16	Promote peaceful and inclusive societies for sustainable development, provide access to justice for all and build effective, accountable and inclusive institutions at all levels.

① A village comprehensive cultural service center is a grassroots public cultural institution with abundant resources that offers comprehensive services for communication and culture, party member education, science popularization, legal education, sports and fitness.

② The honor of "civilized villages and towns" aims to encourage the overall development of villages and towns by creating a sound social and living environment in rural areas, accelerating economic development and modernization of agriculture and rural areas, as well as improving quality of life for residents, among others.

③ The coverage rate of village planning and management refers to the ratio of the number of villages that formulate official village plans to the total number of villages.

④ An integrated service station is a station where village officials assist residents with administrative approvals, public services and utility bill payments. In some areas, the station also serves as an intermediary, where farmers can sell products and buy agricultural equipment.

Continued Table

	Major Rural Revitalization Indicators		Corresponding SDGs with similar objectives/ focus dimensions
16	Proportion of villages where the village Party secretary branch also serves as chairman of the village committee	N/A	
17	Proportion of villages with village rules and regulations	N/A	
18	Proportion of villages with a strong collective economy	SDG 8	Promote sustained, inclusive and sustainable economic growth, full and productive employment and decent work for all
19	Engel's coefficient of rural residents	SDG 1	End poverty in all its forms everywhere
20	Income ratio between urban and rural residents	SDG 10	Reduce inequality within and among countries
21	Tap water coverage in rural areas	SDG 6	Ensure availability and sustainable management of water and sanitation for all
22	Proportion of villages with adequate connecting infrastructure	SDG 9	Build resilient infrastructure, promote inclusive and sustainable industrialization and foster innovation

2.3 Institutional Framework and Policy System for Rural Revitalization

Since the proposal of the rural revitalization strategy, a series of supporting policies for the strategy have been introduced, to provide financial support and legal guarantees (see Figure 2 for details). An institutional framework and policy system is now in place at the national level, laying the foundations for modernizing agriculture and rural areas.

Figure 2: Institutional Framework and Policy System for Rural Revitalization

Financial Support

● In 2020, the General Office of the CPC Central Committee and the General Office of the State Council issued the *Opinions on Adjusfing and Improving the Usage ofLand Sale Revenue to Support Rural Revitalizafion*. These specify insfitufional arrangements on diversifying fundraising methods, establishing long-term mechanisms for stable public investment growth and raising the share of land sale revenues to invest in agriculture and rural areas.

● In 2021, the People's Bank of China and the China Banking and Insurance Regulatory Commission introduced the *Assessment Measures on Financial Insfitufions Serving Rural Revitalizafion*. This directs more financial resources into key areas for rural economic and social development, as well as making specific arrangements to enable financial resources to better support rural revitalization.

Working Mechanism

● Inline with a management system defining clear responsibilifies for officials, China adopted a working mechanism whereby the central leadership makes plans, provincial authorities take responsibility, while city and county authorities ensure implementation.

● The CPC committees and governments of each province, autonomous region and municipality must report to the central committee and State Council on their progress in implemenfing the rural revitalizafion strategy.

Legal Guarantee

● Through the *Regulafions on Rural Work of the Communist Party of China introduced in 2019 and the Rural Revitalizafion Promofion Law* introduced in 2021, effecfive policies, working mechanisms and methods relafing to poverty alleviafion and rural revitalizafion are wrirtten into the Party's regula- fionsand laws.

Source: Authors. Based on the analysis of the following policy documents:

1.The State Council of the People's Republic of China, 31 May 2021, *Policy Document, the Assessment Measures on Financial Institutions Serving Rural Revitalization*(Retrieved from: https://www.gov.cn/ zhengce/zhengceku/2021-06/04/content_5615563.htm)

2.The State Council of the People's Republic of China, 14, Dec 2022, *Policy Documents, General Office of the CPC Central Committee and General Office of the State Council Issue Measures for the Implementation of the Responsibility System for Rural Revitalization(Retrieved from:* https://www.gov.cn/ zhengce/2022-12/14/content_5731828.htm?e qid=894dfc51000167ea000000066462e067)

3.The State Council of the People's Republic of China, 1, Sep 2019, Policy Document, *the Regulations on Rural Work of the CPC* (Retrieved from: https://www.gov.cn/ zhengce/2019-09/01/content_5426319.htm)

4.The National People's of the People's Republic of China, 29, Apr 2021, *the Rural Revitalization Promotion Law*" (Retrieved from: http://www.npc.gov.cn/npc/c2/ c30834/202104/t20210429_311287.html)

In May 2020, the highway leading to Abuloha Village, Wuyi Township, Butuo County, Liangshan Yi Autonomous Prefecture, Sichuan Province, was fully connected.

Source of pictures:National Publicity and Education Center for Rural Revitalization

2.4 Importance of Rural Revitalization to China's Development Strategy

The rural revitalization strategy is encoded in the Constitution of the CPC, reinforcing its importance to the country's future. The strategy complements and mutually reinforces other policy priorities. Its implementation is essential to many of the government's development goals, such as delivering common prosperity, the "dual

circulation" strategy[1], peaking carbon emissions before 2030 and achieving carbon neutrality before 2060, along with China's goal of building an "ecological civilization".[2] This approach is further articulated through the perspectives below.

a) Rural revitalization is an important path to common prosperity. Both rural revitalization and common prosperity aim to satisfy the people's expectations of a better life. As a large agricultural country, with over 500 million rural residents,[3] China cannot achieve common prosperity without a flourishing agricultural sector and affluent rural residents[4].

b) Rural revitalization underpins the "dual circulation" strategy. China aims to steadily improve its resilience by leveraging its vast domestic market . To this end, strengthening domestic consumption and investments are two critical factors. Rural revitalization can thus greatly contribute to this agenda, as it has the potential to raise rural per capita disposable incomes, tapping into underutilized rural consumption.

---

[1] The 'dual circulation' strategy is a key economic strategy proposed by the Chinese government. It aims to foster a new double development dynamic, with the domestic economy and international engagement providing mutual reinforcement, and the former as the mainstay.

[2] The overall requirements for ecological civilization were clarified at the18th National Congress of the CPC in 2012. It has been written into China's Constitution and serves as a guiding goal for the country's environmental policies.

[3] National Bureau of Statistics (2021, May 11). *Communiqué of the Seventh National Population Census (No. 7)*. National Bureau of Statistics of China. Retrieved from: http://www.stats.gov.cn/english/PressRelease/202105/t20210510_1817192.html

[4] Qi, Z., Jiakun, Z., Shunqiang, L., & Mei, K. (2022). Scientific Connotation, Inner Relationship and Strategic Key Points of Rural Revitalization under the Goal of Common Prosperity. *Journal of Northwest University (Philosophy and Social Sciences Edition)*, 52(03), 44-53.

c) Rural revitalization is key to achieving China's targets of peaking carbon emissions before 2030 and achieving carbon neutrality before 2060, as well as realizing China's goal of building an "ecological civilization".

The major battlefields of conserving energy and reducing carbon emissions lie in the industrial, energy and transport sectors. Although greenhouse gas (GHG) emissions from agriculture make up only modest proportion of total emissions, the role of the agricultural sector in China's progress to its climate goals is not negligible, as it also involves carbon sink systems with vast carbon sequestration capabilities.[1] In addition, rural areas are blessed with rich natural resources, making them important fronts for building China's ecological civilization. Consequently, promoting green, eco-friendly and low-carbon agriculture will help in achieving carbon peaking and neutrality targets, as well as an ecological civilization.

---

[1]   Ministry of Ecology and Environment (2019 July 1). *Key Statistics from China Second Biennial Update Report on Climate Change.* Ministry of Ecology and Environment of People's Republic of China. Retrieved from: https://www.mee.gov.cn/ywgz/ydqhbh/wsqtkz/201907/t20190701_708248. shtml

3

Revitalization of Rural Industry

3.1 Significance of Revitalizing Rural Industries

The scope of rural industries encompasses traditional and new industries, as well as the integration of primary, secondary and tertiary industries in rural areas. Revitalizing them involves raising their quality and increasing the benefits that they generate, improving the industrial system, optimizing their employment structure and better supporting their integrated development, which can expand income-generating opportunities in rural areas.

3.2 Policy Framework for Revitalizing Rural Industries

Industrial revitalization is the cornerstone of China's rural revitalization strategy. China has been improving the policy system and framework for industrial development since the 18th National Congress in 2012. In 2019, the State Council introduced the *Guiding Opinions of the State Council on Promoting Revitalization of Rural Industries*, which systematically explains the concept of revitalizing rural industry and relevant key actions. The Ministry of Agriculture and Rural Affairs (MARA) promulgated the *National Rural Industry Development Plan (2020—2025) in 2020 and Guiding Opinions on Diversifying Functions of Agriculture for High-quality Development of Rural Industries* in 2021. Policies for rural industrial development have been improved and are now

an important component of overall policies for strengthening agriculture and benefiting rural people.

In the remainder of this section, a few select examples of supporting policies are presented.

a) Preferential Fiscal and Tax Policies: Since the 18th National Congress in 2012, China has been improving policies to boost agriculture and support the rural population, promoting more financial investment in agriculture, rural areas and rural people. Guarantees for rural fiscal budgets and support for rural industries have been strengthened. Policies have encouraged local funds to flow to rural industries and have required that more revenues from land sales be spent on agriculture, as well as the rural industrial sector. Local governments with suitable conditions have been encouraged to set up rural industrial development funds through market-oriented approaches, with a focus on technological innovation . They have also been encouraged to provide subsidies to agricultural enterprises that employ rural residents with disabilities and labor from poor rural households, along with implementing relevant preferential tax policies.

b) Financial Service Policies for Rural Areas: Since 2012, each year's No.1 Central Document[1] has specified requirements and made plans to strengthen rural financial services. The *Guiding Opinions of the State Council on Promoting Revitalization of Rural*

---

[1]   The No. 1 Central Document is the first policy document of each year issued in January by the Central Committee of the CPC and the State Council. For the last two decades,it has focused on rural development issues.

In September 2020, at the e-commerce service center in Yecheng County, Kashgar Prefecture, Xinjiang Uyghur Autonomous Region, two local bloggers are live streaming on the social medias, selling walnuts and their processed products.

Source of pictures:National Publicity and Education Center for Rural Revitalization

Industries makes clear that the government should guide county-level financial institutions to channel the deposits they absorb towards local development, particularly to local rural industries. Preferential policies for fundraising for small and micro businesses also apply to rural industries, innovation and entrepreneurship. The state also makes full use of the national agricultural credit guarantee system, which assists local authorities in supporting agricultural and rural industry credit guarantees, through measures such as guarantee fee subsidies and business bonuses. Under the system, the scope of collateral is expanded to allow farmers to mortgage

agricultural facilities and machinery, as well as their contracted land use rights where there is clear ownership. Fundraising guarantees for rural industries have been reinforced. Local governments are encouraged to issue general bonds to support public welfare projects directed towards rural revitalization and special bonds to complete any financing gaps, to aid qualified, profit-generating, rural public welfare projects.

c) **Policies on the Participation of Private Capital:** Introducing private capital, where relevant, can potentially ease the debt burden and fiscal pressure on the government, while bringing direct and indirect benefits to enterprises. *The Guiding Opinions of the State Council on Promoting Revitalization of Rural Industries states* that industrial and commercial capital should be guided in an orderly fashion to invest in or start rural industries that local people can easily participate in and benefit from. Local governments will provide occupational training and employment services to attract and support enterprises, to promote local industrial development. MARA and the National Administration for Rural Revitalization (NARR) promulgated the *Guidelines on Private Capital Investment in Agriculture and Rural Areas* in 2020, 2021 and 2022. These Guidelines identify 13 key industries and fields in which private capital is encouraged to invest. It also outlines five models in which private capital could contribute to rural development, including promoting full industrial chain development, exploring opportunities for overall regional development, innovating public-private partnership, establishing rural revitalization investment

funds and strengthening benefit-sharing mechanisms.

d) Supporting Policies for Rural Land Used towards Industrial Development. When making the annual plan for land use, greater support is given to the development of rural industries by allocating more land for this purpose. Laws and regulations related to this are being revised and improved, with reforms being made to bring rural collective construction land onto the market, which will increase the supply of land for rural industries. Management of idle rural land that belongs to counties and villages has been strengthened. This landis intended primarily for new rural industries and new forms of business, along with for those who return or move to the countryside to start businesses or engage in other innovative activities.

3.3 Achievements in Revitalizing Rural Industries

The development of modern agriculture is accelerating. Guaranteeing national food security is the top priority in developing high-quality, modern agriculture. In this respect, the total grain output in China reached 682 million tonnes in 2021, marking the seventh consecutive year above the Government's target of 650 million tonnes. The total output of grain rose further in 2022 to 686 million tonnes.[1]

---

[1] *China National Bureau of Statistics (2023). Statistical Communique of the People's Republic of China on the 2022 National Economic and Social Development.* Retrieved from: http://www.stats. gov.cn/english/PressRelease/202302/t20230227_1918979.html

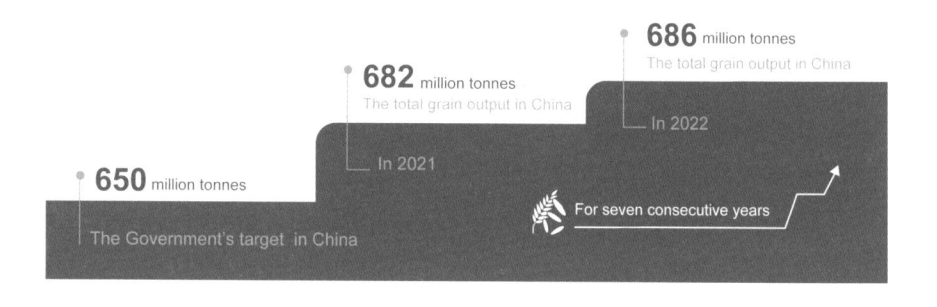

Agricultural infrastructure has significantly improved, particularly regarding prime farmland.[1] The country has upgraded over 600,000 km2 of land as prime farmland and implemented a conservation program for chernozem soils.

Next-generation information and communication technology (ICT) has been used in agricultural production, operations, management and services. Statistics from the National Development and Reform Commission (NDRC) in 2021 indicate that the contribution rate of science and technology to growth of gross output in agriculture reached 61 percent, up 3.5 percentage points from 2017. Further, more than 72 percent of crop ploughing, planting and harvesting was mechanized, up 6 percentage points from 2017.

Rural industry is steadily diversifying, through the development of numerous different industries, including services and rural tourism. In 2021, leisure agriculture and rural tourism made great strides. The number of leisure farms, agricultural parks and agri-

---

[1]   Prime farmland is level, fertile and contiguous land well-supported with modern amenities. It enjoys a sound ecology and is highly resilient. Inline with modern agricultural production and management, it ensures stable and high yields even in times of drought or excessive rain.

entertainment facilities in China surpassed 300,000, generating an annual operational income of more than RMB 700 billion (USD 100 billion). In the same year, national rural online retail sales reached RMB 2.05 trillion (USD 293 billion), while leisure agriculture and rural tourism catered for more than 2.9 billion visitors.

There have been many innovative developments in the rural services industry, particularly regarding e-commerce. Over 30,000 e-commerce stations involving agriculture businesses achieved online sales of rural products of RMB 1.3 trillion in 2021 (USD 186 billion), of which RMB 300 billion (USD 43 billion) came from agricultural products.[1]

There has been a significant shift towards rural industrial integration. "Agriculture plus" models integrating agriculture with culture, education, tourism, health and wellness, along with information technology, are developing fast.

Cooperation and benefits-sharing mechanisms are improving. According to statistics from MARA, as the country encourages cooperation between enterprises and farmers, more than 100 million farmers have signed contracts with leading enterprises in agricultural industrialization. A government report shows that contracted farmers can earn 50 percent more than their uncontracted

---

[1] Statistics released from the conference of implementation of The Rural Revitalization Strategy (2018—2022) held by the NDRC on September 28, 2022.

counterparts.[①] Profit dividend models are promoted to help farmers raise and sustain higher incomes. These models include order purchase + dividend;[②] guaranteed return + dividend based on shareholding;[③] and land rent + labor salary + sales bonus.[④] Agricultural industrialization cooperatives have been built through cooperation based on shareholdings. These have a clear division of work and responsibilities, taking advantage of complementary strengths, as well as sharing risks and benefits.

Innovation and entrepreneurship are growing. China has built nearly 2,200 innovation and entrepreneurship parks and incubation training bases in rural areas, encouraging 11.2 million people to move or return to the countryside to launch startups or engage in other innovative activities. On average, each entity provides full-time jobs for six to seven people, along with flexible employment opportunities for 15 to 20 people[⑤].

[①] Changfu, H. (2019, April 21). *The State Council's Report on Rural Industry Development.* The National People's Congress of the People's Republic of China. http://www. npc.gov.cn/zgrdw/npc/xinwen/2019-04/21/content_2085626.htm

[②] Order purchase + dividend: In this model, an enterprise buys the product from the farmers for onward sales or processing and pays them an annual dividend based on overall profit.

[③] Guaranteed return plus dividend based on shareholding: In this model, the farmers own shares in a collective enterprise. The enterprise buys their output at a fixed rate and pays them an annual dividend based on their shareholding.

[④] Land rent, labor salary, + sales bonus: In this model, an enterprise rents the farmers' land from them, pays them a salary to work the land and grants them a sales bonus for their products.

[⑤] See Footnote 27

Special Column 1:

Promoting Green Development of the Fruit Industry:

A Specialized Cooperative for Fruit Farmers of Longguang Village (Nanjiang Township,Guizhou Province)

Longguang Village, in Nanjiang Township, Kaiyang County, Gúiyang City, Guizhou Province, is a prolific source of loquats. In 2014, Tao Qiuyun went back to Longguang, his hometown and launched a specialized cooperative for fruit farmers. At that time, the average household income of a local loquat farmer was only about RMB 8,000/ Annum (USD 1,150). In just a few years, the orchards of Longguang Village have expanded from a few acres to almost 7 km^2, with many fruit varieties. The cooperative has registered trademarks and created a high-quality brand offering pollution-free and fully traceable fruit. Thanks to e-commerce, Longguang loquats are now sold nationwide. Furthermore, the vigorous development of the fruit industry boosted rural tourism in the county. In 2021, the average household income in Longguang Village rose to RMB 21,000/Annum (USD 3,000). Tao Qiuyun has not only transformed his own life, but also created a path to prosperity for the village.

a) Building a Service Platform that Focuses on the Whole Industrial Chain

The cooperative was launched by 11 farming households in Longguang Village, with the goal of expanding the scale and standardizing the development of the local loquat industry. By 2016, its membership had grown to 43 households, reaching 113 one year later. As a service platform, the cooperative is in constant contact with industries, farmers and experts, carrying out product research and development, expanding

the market and serving its members. The cooperative organizes regular meetings for members to discuss development plans and explore solutions to problems that arise in production and sales. After several years, the cooperative has developed a standardized operation model characterized by unified management, quality technology, structured procurement, scientific pest control, price management, acquisition, branding, marketing and e-commerce.

b) Focusing on Product Quality and Enhancing the Loquat Brand's Added Value

The cooperative keeps strict control over product quality. In the production process, requirements for agricultural product safety supervision are rigorous. Fertilizers and pesticides are used on a rational and scientific basis – regular samples are taken and sent to the agricultural supervision authorities for testing. The cooperative also requires members to sign a security commitment document for internal scrutiny, so that products can be traced back to the individual source. In addition, it focuses on regional brand-building, reinforcing product traceability. Longguang Village has succeeded in aligning its production base with the market. The cooperative now plans to extend the industrial chain to deep processing, to add further value.

c) Growing More Fruit Varieties and Diversifying Sales Channels

Since the cooperative was established, the region has undergone a change from scattered planting under different standards, to nearly 7 km^2 of orchards covering three villages. To overcome a bottleneck particular to agricultural industrial development – whereby farmers' incomes fail to grow in parallel with higher output – the cooperative has adopted an integrated online and offline sales model. In 2021, they cooperated with fruit wholesale markets and supermarket fruit distributors in Beijing,

Shenzhen, Shanghai, Kunming and other cities, selling more than 100 tons of loquats. In addition, they took advantage of the opportunity provided by a rich local resource – the Ten-Mile Gallery[①] – to organize fruit picking and other leisure activities for tourists. To ensure continued development, the cooperative commits 2 percent of its profits as a rolling fund for product packaging development, members' technical training, marketing and other related activities.

[①] The Ten-Mile Gallery is the local tourism area consisting of more than 10 villages in Hefeng Town and Nanjiang Town along the Qinglong River, where tourists can enjoy local scenery and engage in agricultural-themed activities.

3.4 Challenges in Revitalizing Rural Industries

Low added-value of agricultural products: capacities for scientific and technological innovation in rural enterprises are relatively weak, especially in agricultural product processing, where technology lags behind those of developed countries. Rural industries still mainly supply roughly processed products with low added-value, lacking targeted and mid-to-high-end products and services, thus creating limited brand premiums.

Most agribusinesses are scattered, with only 28 percent located in industrial parks, resulting in limited economies of scale[①]. Some regions and industries pursue expansions in scale and volume without careful planning, resulting in ineffective supply, intensified competition, as well as declines in quality and efficiency. As some agricultural industries expand, there is also a risk that production might move from suitable areas, to less suitable or even unsuitable locations, leading to lower quality products and a loss of competitiveness,

① See Footnote 27

possibly harming their branding and reputation.

Limited financial flows: rural industries depend heavily on public funds, with rural finance largely insufficient. Selective lending by rural financial institutions is a common practice, and there is a growing trend of financial resources leaning towards urban, rather than rural areas. Furthermore, there are limited business models that can turn rural resources into cash flows. Therefore, private capital remains reluctant to venture into rural industries.

Inadequate rural industrial infrastructure, leading to high operational and logistics costs. Some villages do not have adequate supplies of water, electricity and gas. Additionally, transport routes, networks and communications facilities, along with logistics and warehousing infrastructure, do not yet cover all rural areas in China. Additionally, some facilities are not well-established, such as wholesale markets in places of origin, platforms that connect products and markets, as well as direct sales outlets for fresh farm produce.

4

Human Capital Revitalization

4.1 Significance of Rural Human Capital Revitalization

The revitalization of human capital in rural areas aims at enhancing human capital for implementing China's rural revitalization strategy. As distinct from ordinary rural laborers, "rural capital resources" refers to groups with professional knowledge or skills working in, or serving the countryside, contributing to rural development and playing leading roles in it.

One of the key challenges facing rural development in China is the persistent loss of human resources in the countryside. Young or middle-aged residents and high-caliber workers continue to flow out of rural areas, leaving behind an inadequate workforce, as well as an aging population. Data shows that the number of migrant workers in China totaled 172 million in 2021, rising by 2.13 million over the previous year. The average age of migrant workers was 36.8 years; 17.1 percent had received junior college education or above. Rural residents who migrate to cities are mostly young, with relatively higher education levels than those staying behind.[1]

As China pushes ahead its rural revitalization strategy – accelerating modernization of agriculture and rural areas – the imbalance

---

[1] National Bureau of Statistics (2022, April 19). *Report on Migrant Workers 2021.* National Bureau of Statistics of China. Retrieved from: http://www.stats.gov.cn/xxgk/sjfb/ zxfb2020/202204/ t20220429_1830139.html

between supply and demand of skilled workers and professionals is a key area that needs to be addressed. Therefore, invigorating rural human resources and supporting a wide range of workforce skills are both requirements of the central government and ways of meeting urgent, practical needs at the grassroots level.

To encourage talented individuals of all types to participate in rural development, in 2021 the General Office of the CPC Central Committee and the General Office of the State Council issued the *Opinions on Accelerating the Revitalization of Rural Human Capital.* This document classifies rural human resources into five categories: agricultural production and management, secondary and tertiary industry development, rural public services, rural governance, as well as agricultural science and technology.

The first two are also collectively referred to as rural industrial human resources (Figure 4).

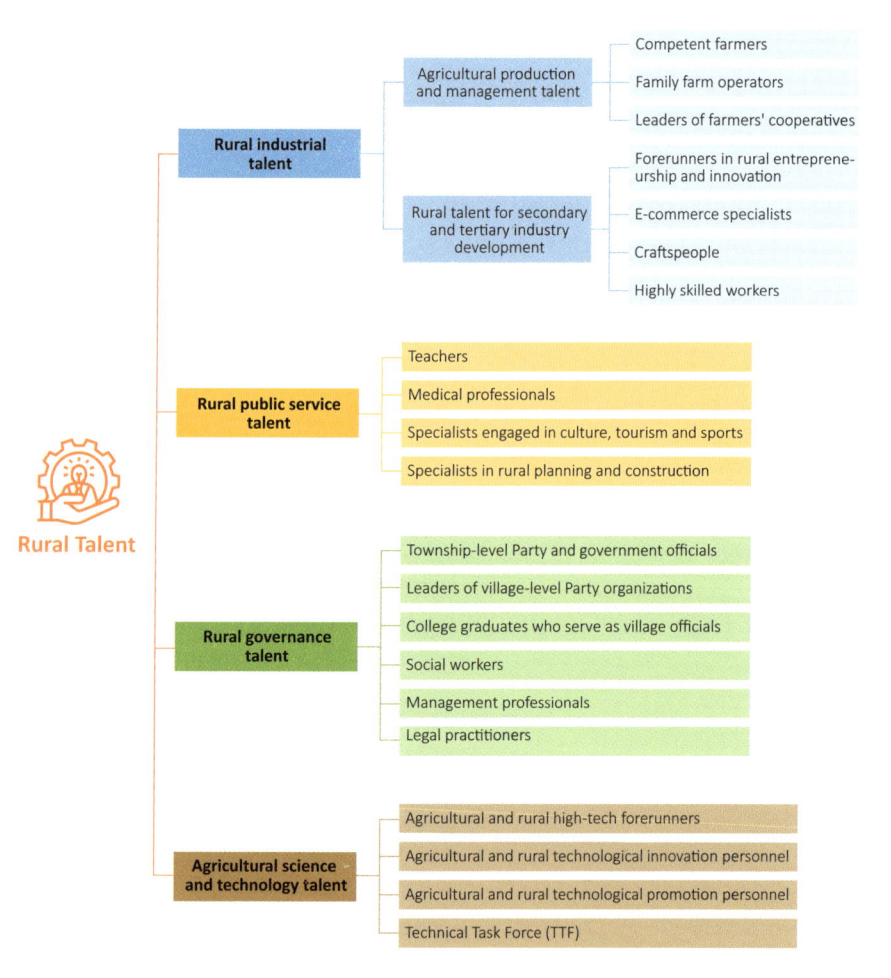

Figure 4: Categories of rural human capital①

① The State Council of the People's Republic of China, (23, Feb 2021), *General Office of the CPC Central Committee and General Office of the State Council issued the Opinions on Accelerating the Revitalization of Rural Talents.* Retrieved from: https://www.gov.cn/zhengce/2021-02/23/content_5588496.htm

4.2 Policies and Actions in Promoting Rural Human Capital Revitalization

To effectively retain and attract human resources for rural development, China has implemented a series of policies and measures to progressively expand its rural human resources pool, including providing targeted education and training opportunities, creating incentives for talented individuals to remain in or return to rural areas, while promoting entrepreneurship and innovation in rural areas.

4.2.1 Policy arrangements for rural human capital revitalization

1) Fostering rural human capital

A key part of the strategy is to provide education and training opportunities to equip rural residents with the skills they need to participate in the modern economy. Targeted trainings are designed for different types of human resources.

Box 1. Rural human capital

Rural industrial human capital: The success of rural industries hinges upon people with high- value knowledge and skills. Specifically, farmers who are trained, skilled in business operations and management, with technical expertise, are the core force for farming the land and ensuring food production and security. Family farms and farmer cooperatives are important components of the new agricultural management entities. As forerunners in rural entrepreneurship and innovation, rural e-commerce

specialists, craftspeople, as well as highly-skilled workers, are expected to promote rural innovation and sustained economic development.

Rural public service human capital: To elevate basic public services in rural areas and achieve parity in this regard with urban areas, support for rural public service human resources, including teachers and medical workers, is essential.

Rural governance human capital: As "front-line forces" for grassroots governance, rural governance human resources includes two categories: 1) Township-level Party and government officials, leaders of village-level Party organizations, as well as college graduates serving as village officials responsible for carrying out policies relating to agriculture, rural areas and rural people; 2) Professionals from various fields, such as rural social workers, management professionals and legal practitioners. They play an important role in building rural social relationships, improving community social management, along with ensuring rural residents' access to public legal services.

Agricultural science and technology human capital: Human resources in agricultural science and technology is the pillar for technological innovation and high-quality development. Agricultural innovation human resources refers to people who provide cutting-edge scientific and technological support to rural industries and undertakings, through continuous research and development, as well as by introducing and applying new technologies. The Technical Task Force (TTF) includes professional and technical personnel selected and assigned by local CPC committees and governments to solve issues related to agriculture, rural areas and rural people. They engage in commercializing scientific and technological achievements, developing competitive and specialty

industries, along with building agricultural science and technology parks, as well as industrial bases, to meet market demand and the needs of rural people.

a) Fostering professional farmers

First of all, China attaches great importance to cultivating professional farmers. According to China's *Development Plan for the Cultivation of New-type Professional Farmers Across China during the 13th Five- Year Plan Period* issued in 2017, the country intends to speed up the creation of professional farmers who are well-educated, knowledgeable about agricultural technology, as well as skilled in operations and management. The plan also supports agriculture-related vocational colleges by providing farmers with formal schooling, and sets out to create an integrated, digital platform at national, provincial and county- level, to better train these professionals.

To further promote entrepreneurship, China is increasing support to founders of new agricultural business entities. In 2017, China issued the *Opinions on Accelerating the Construction of Relevant Systems to Foster New Agricultural Business Entities,* specifying that support will be given to those who lead new agri-businesses, while promoting extensive training for such leaders across the country. In Shandong Province, for example, training in agricultural skills, operations, management and other areas is provided both online and offline.

Skills training is also being provided to improve the competitiveness of those who pursue opportunities in non-agricultural sectors within rural areas. MARA launched training programs on practical skills and delivered specialized training courses on e-commerce related to agriculture. Guangdong Province has also launched successful skills training programs for other groups of rural workers, including chefs, domestic service providers and technicians.

b) Attracting new human capital to the countryside

Introducing external talent to rural areas is equally important. To achieve this, China has implemented several policies and established platforms encouraging people to return to their rural hometowns and start businesses.

The government has been consistently promoting this idea since 2015, when the General Office of the State Council issued the *Implementation Opinions on Encouraging Migrant Workers and Other Personnel to Return to Hometowns and Start Businesses.* The Guideline calls on migrant workers, college graduates, decommissioned military personnel and others to return to their hometowns in rural areas to work, or to start businesses. The NDRC, together with relevant departments, has organized many pilot projects since then to encourage this. To further strengthen policy support, the Ministry of Human Resources and Social Security (MOHRSS) and two other departments jointly issued the *Opinions on Further Encouraging Human resource to Return or Come to the Countryside to Start Businesses* in 2019.

Additionally, China has established platforms to support these returnees, building a talent ecosystem. In 2021, MARA issued the *Catalogue of National Rural Entrepreneurship Parks (Bases) 2021*, introducing 2,210 rural entrepreneurship parks and bases that provide large carrying capacities, a wide range of functions and quality services. The aim is to encourage more people to move or return to the countryside to start businesses. The MOHRSS has built more than 8,800 entrepreneurship carriers, such as startup incubators and entrepreneurship parks for returnees, providing low-cost, convenient incubation services for prospective entrepreneurs moving or returning to the countryside.

c) Innovative ways for urban human capital to serve in rural areas
To address the human resources gap in rural areas, especially in delivering public services, the government has established a system for coordinated use of trained professionals in counties that allows for more flexible employment arrangements. For instance, specialists employed by counties can be assigned to work in townships, and those employed by townships can be dispatched to work in villages. Furthermore, specific programs targeting three different types of human resources have been developed.

Firstly, several programs are in place to encourage urban-based educators to serve in rural areas.

For instance, under the state training program for special posts co-implemented by the Ministry of Education and Ministry of Finance (MOF), college graduates are selected through open recruitment to teach in poor rural schools in central and western regions for a three-year period. During their service, they are paid out of special funds in accordance with national wage standards. In 2022, there were 67,000 such teaching posts.

Source of pictures:National Publicity and Education Center for Rural Revitalization

Secondly, capacities of grassroots medical and health service institutions continue to improve, supported by match-making personnel from urban areas.

China has strengthened the ranks of medical and health service professionals in rural areas, by launching tuition-free and targeted training programs for medical undergraduates, assistant general practitioners and leading doctors in county-level hospitals. [1]In 2021, medical schools from central and western regions

---

① Tuition-free and targeted training for medical undergraduates is a special enrollment program in the national college entrance exam. Undergraduates in this program will receive free education and accommodation, as well as enjoy living allowances during their study term, if they sign a contract to serve in grassroots medical institutions for six years.

admitted 6,280 undergraduate medical students into their targeted training programs and trained 6,960 assistant general practitioners, thus ensuring a steady supply of medical professionals to rural

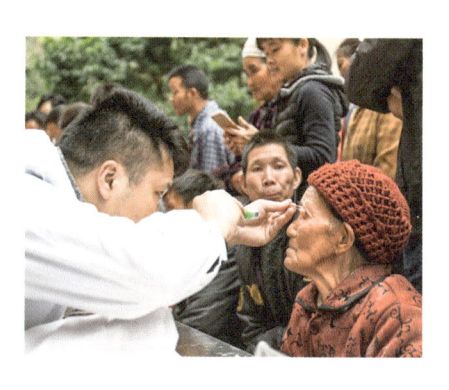

area facilities. In the same year, a program was also initiated to encourage retired doctors to provide medical services for rural communities, maximizing the potential of retirees. In 2021, 529 institutions and 139 medical personnel registered for this program.

Source of pictures:National Publicity and Education Center for Rural Revitalization

Thirdly, science and technology professionals are encouraged to work in rural areas, in support of rural revitalization.

The Ministry of Science and Technology (MOST) operates the TTF program, along with a special program assigning technical

professionals, including prioritizing ethnic minority areas and border regions . In 2021, MOST sent 18,072 technicians to 22 central and western provinces and cities, where they provided training for 3,534 local people.

Source of pictures:National Publicity and Education Center for Rural Revitalization

4.2.2 Creating an enabling environment for rural human capital revitalization

To ensure that China's rural revitalization strategy is implemented smoothly and strengthen cross-ministry cooperation, the Chinese government has launched a cross-ministry working mechanism that includes relevant departments, coordinated by the rural working group of the CPC Committee. With support from this working group, "A guideline on accelerating the revitalization of rural human capital" was jointly issued by the Central Committee of CPC and the State Council in 2021. In addition, rural human capital revitalization has been included as a performance indicator for overall rural revitalization . China also encourages systematic, regulated and consistent human resource development in relation to agriculture, rural areas and rural people, by cementing investment in rural human resource revitalization, building related platforms, formulating special planning, as well as improving rural infrastructure and public services.

a) Funding support for rural human capital

The government provides subsidies and preferential policies to those who start businesses in their hometowns, including entrepreneurship and loan interest subsidies. In 2021, the General Office of the CPC Central Committee and the General Office of the State Council promulgated *Opinions on Accelerating the Revitalization of Rural Human Resources*. This requires creating subsidy policies for people experiencing harsh living conditions while working in rural and remote areas, so as to grant higher

Villagers of Huaxi Village are discussing the village poverty alleviation and development plan.

Source of pictures:National Publicity and Education Center for Rural Revitalization

incomes to township officials than their counterparts in government bodies at the county-level. Local governments also provide their own subsidies. Changsha city in Hunan province, for example, grants respective one-time subsidies of RMB 3,000, 5,000, and 10,000 to those who are recognized as junior, intermediate and senior new-model professional farmers.

b) Public service guarantee for rural human capital

In 2020, nine ministries, including MARA, jointly issued the *Opinions on Deepening the Cultivation of Rural Innovation and Entrepreneurship Leaders,* which call for accelerating the establishment of a nationwide, unified social insurance public service platform. This platform seeks to provide an efficient transfer and continuation of social insurance relationships for rural innovation and entrepreneurship leaders. In 2022, MARA introduced the *Development Plan for Building Human Resource Teams in Agriculture and Rural Areas during the 14*th *Five-Year Plan.* This encourages local governments to remove policy barriers

in education, medical services, social security and public services between rural and urban areas, to encourage human resources to remain in rural areas.

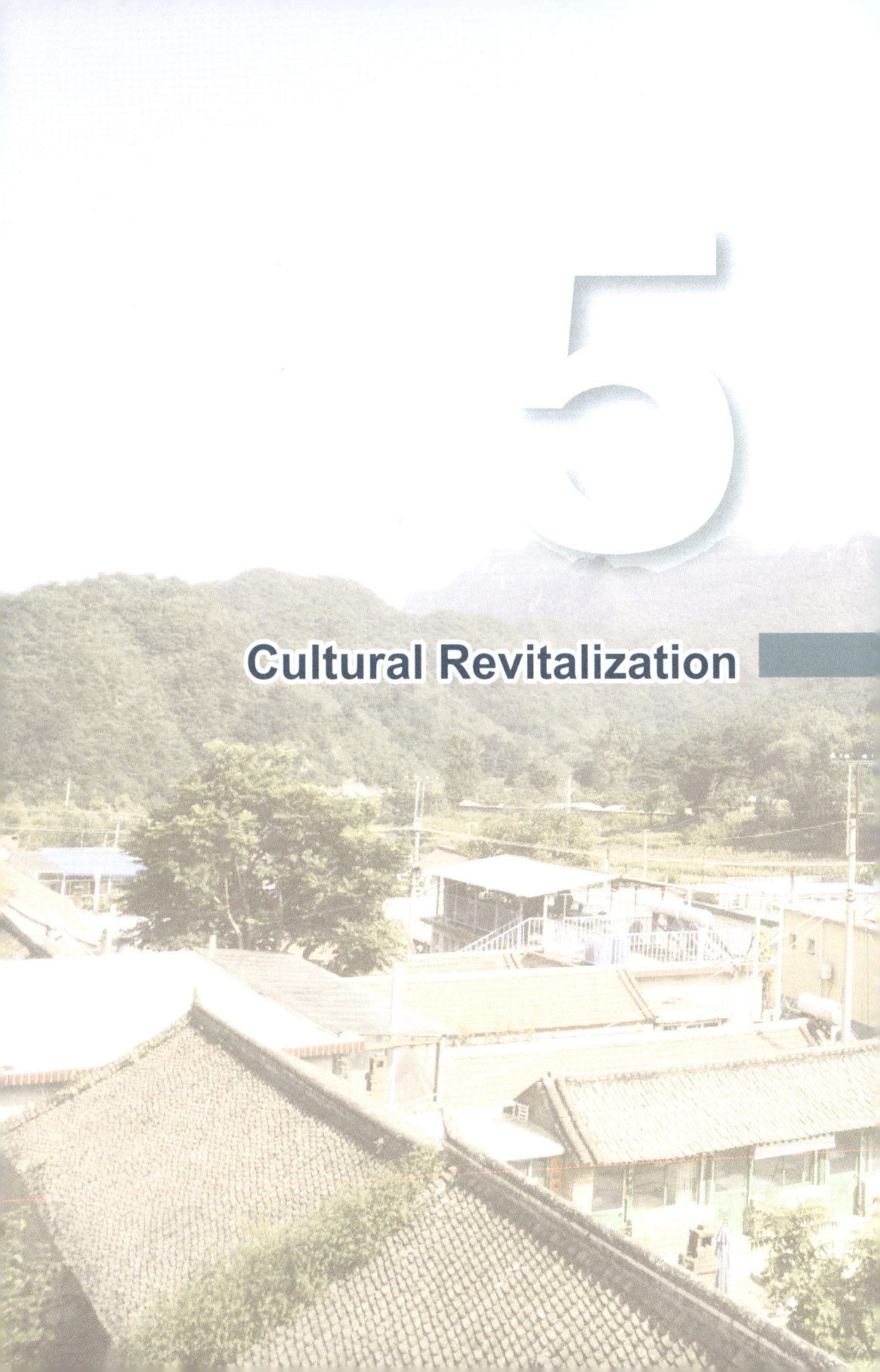

5

Cultural Revitalization

5.1 Significance of Cultural Revitalization

Perceived as the root and soul of the Chinese people, Chinese traditions and local culture are a vital intangible asset. If utilized appropriately, they can serve as a driving force for rural development, a resource to enrich rural residents' intellectual and cultural lives, as well as promoting a cultured and harmonious social environment, as highlighted in the primary targets of rural revitalization. Cultural revitalization comprises two major elements:

Firstly, through the inheritance and protection of traditional culture, cultural revitalization aims to harness local cultures to develop cultural industries and tourism, along with leveraging the market value of rural cultural resources, while nurturing rural culture in return.

Secondly, cultural revitalization is dedicated to providing quality intellectual and cultural services to meet the ever-increasing expectations of rural residents. To this end, modern cultural facilities should be established taking local conditions into account, while enhancing access through digital technologies. In addition, publicity campaigns are being launched to help combat unhealthy customs and activities[1], as well as to motivate rural residents

---

[1] Xiaowen, W., & Jimin, L. (2021). The theoretical quality of the great poverty alleviation spirit and the practical expression of rural revitalization, *Gansu Theory Research,* 267(5), 13-18+2.

participating in rural governance[1].

5.2 Critical Measures in Support of Cultural Revitalization

5.2.1 Financial support

Since 2015, the central government has established a series of fiscal subsidies to aid the development of local public cultural services. Amounts of the fiscal subsidies have fluctuated over the years. In 2021, the central government provided RMB 15.2 billion (2.2 billion USD) to support the local public cultural service system, roughly the same amount as the previous year. The purpose of these subsidies is to guide and support local authorities in providing basic public cultural services, improving public cultural facilities and expanding the cultural human resource pool at the grassroots level. It also intends to accelerate development of a modern public cultural service system, as well as facilitate standardization and equal accessibility of basic public cultural services. Those subsidies guarantee basic rights to the public, such as reading books and newspapers, watching TV programs, enjoying movies, appreciating art, as well as engaging in cultural and sporting activities.

To improve the financial support mechanism, the General Office of the State Council issued the *Guiding Opinions of the State Council on Advancing the Reform of the Division of Financial Powers and Expenditure Responsibilities between the Central and*

---

[1]   Chengmin, H. (2021). The contemporary value of rural revitalization, *Red Flag Manuscript*, (23), 29-32+1.

In June 2020, students in Jinxiu Yao Autonomous County, Laibin City, Guangxi Zhuang Autonomous Region are taking artificial intelligence courses.

Source of pictures:National Publicity and Education Center for Rural Revitalization

the Local Governments in the Domain of Public Culture in 2020. This document clarifies that free access to public cultural facilities is a responsibility shared by the central and local governments. It also defines the standards and ratios of basic subsidies provided by the central government. Additionally, MOF and relevant central government departments have jointly established a management process for public cultural services, covering the entire chain of fund allocation, budget implementation and performance evaluation. Indicators reflecting the protection of people's basic cultural rights and interests, such as residents' satisfaction with their ability to participate in cultural activities, have been selected to assess local governments' performance in providing cultural services. Funds will be allocated by the central government based on local performance to further encourage local governments and

departments of culture and tourism to improve the quality of their public cultural services.

5.2.2 Improving the rural public cultural service system

Three main policy documents are relevant here:

1. The *Cultural and Tourist Development Plan during the 14th Five-Year Plan Period and the Public Cultural Service System Building Plan during the 14th Five-Year Plan Period,* released by the Ministry of Culture and Tourism (MCT) . Both documents prioritize creating an integrated urban and rural public cultural service system. They also require efforts to remedy shortcomings at the grassroots level and coordinate development in urban and rural areas to narrow the gap in public cultural services.

2. In 2021, the MCT, NDRC and MOF jointly released *Guiding Opinions on Enhancing the Quality Development of Public Cultural Services* . The document puts forward nine concrete steps, including standardizing public cultural services, improving the grassroots public cultural service network, expanding public cultural spaces in rural and urban areas, along with increasing the quality and efficiency of public cultural services.

3. Regarding standards, *the National Standards for Basic Public Services (2021 Version)* was issued jointly by the NDRC, the Publicity Department of the CPC Central Committee and other departments. It clarifies the eight major features of China's basic public cultural services: free access to public cultural

facilities; bringing traditional Chinese opera performances to rural communities; access to movies, to books and newspapers, to radio and television broadcasts; ensuring cultural services for ethnic minorities; as well as providing cultural and sports services for people with disabilities . The document also specifies the recipients, contents, standards, responsibilities and leading departments relative to each service. It provides an important base for governments at all levels to deliver their respective duties and for people to enjoy their corresponding cultural rights.

In May 2018, villagers in Dashiling Village, Shangen Town, Wanning City, Hainan Province, read in a rural bookstore jointly built by the village.

Source of pictures:National Publicity and Education Center for Rural Revitalization

5.2.3 Protect and leverage rural culture heritage

In terms of rural cultural inheritance and protection, the Opinions

of the Central Committee of the CPC and the State Council for Comprehensively Promoting Rural Revitalization and Accelerating the Modernization of Agriculture and Rural Areas, also known as the No. 1 Central Document for 2021, calls for stronger guidance on defining features of the countryside and protecting traditional houses, along with historical and cultural towns and villages. It also demands greater efforts to preserve cultural heritage and relics in rural areas. Since 2012, the former Ministry of Agriculture has been sponsoring fieldwork to identify important areas and features of Chinese agricultural heritage.

To enrich the rural cultural industries, the MCT released the *Plan of Cultural Industry Development during the 14th Five-Year Plan Period.* This proposes actions to build a number of towns and villages characterized by unique cultural industries, as well as to facilitate the blending of rural cultural features and traditional techniques with innovative designs, modern technologies and new trends. Examples include agricultural leisure products, agricultural museums, museums of village history, agricultural handicraft products, Chinese folk-art performances, traditional festival celebrations and rural cultural products based on agricultural tools.

5.2.4 Discourage undesirable rural customs and activities

The No. 1 Central Document of 2021 further specifies the requirements for raising cultural and ethical standards in rural areas . Efforts should be stepped up to discourage undesirable rural customs and activities and do away with unhealthy behaviors and

traditions. Examples may include excessive dowries, extravagance and waste on social events such as weddings and funerals, households obsessively trying to outdo each other in "generosity", as well as feudal superstitions. In 2020 and 2021, MARA organized 46 promotional campaigns for exemplary cases of civil and cultured social behavior in rural villages.

5.3 Achievements in Cultural Revitalization

In China's rural areas, notable achievements have been made in cultural inheritance and preservation, developing cultural industries and creating a cultured and civil social environment. These successes have vastly enriched the spiritual and cultural lives of rural residents.

5.3.1 Rural residents' consumption of cultural and entertaining products is growing steadily

Rural residents' cultural spending in China is growing steadily, with rural per capita consumption of education, culture and entertainment in 2021 climbing by 25.7 percent year-on-year, to RMB 1,645. Rural tourism in China also continues to grow, albeit slower than in urban areas, according to data from *the Statistical Communiqué of the People's Republic of China on the 2021 National Economic and Social Development.* In 2021, China's domestic tourists reached 3.25 billion, rising by 12.8 percent year-on-year. Urban areas received 2.34 billion total tourists, a 13.4 percent increase, while rural areas saw 900 million tourists, climbing by 11.1 percent.

5.3.2 Infrastructure for rural culture and sports activities is improving

More integrated cultural service centers have been built in grassroots communities. By the end of 2021, more than 570 thousand integrated cultural service centers had opened at village and community levels, covering almost all rural areas.[①] About 94 percent of counties, cities and districts in China have set up a network of cultural centers (providing 32 thousand branches) and 93 percent of counties, cities and districts have established a system[②] of libraries (providing 49 thousand branches).[③]

Radio and television infrastructure have also improved. In 2021, the rural radio broadcasting coverage rate was 99.3 percent, while the television broadcasting rate was 99.5 percent. According to the China Internet Network Information Center, all administrative villages are equipped with Internet infrastructure and enjoy broadband services. As of June 2021, there were 297 million rural

---

[①] The integrated cultural service includes the provision of entertainment performances, newspapers, radio and television, film screenings, cultural and sports activities, exhibitions and trainings.

[②] On December 29, 2016, the Ministry of Culture, the State Administration of Press, Publication, Radio, Film and Television, the General Administration of Sport, the NDRC and the MOF issued a notice on printing and releasing Guidelines on building central-branch systems of libraries and cultural centers at county-level. The *Guideline* pointed out that creating such a system is critical to building a modern public cultural service system. It also represents a drive for more efficient integration of public cultural resources, better public cultural services and higher quality cultural resources towards grassroots communities.

[③] Ministry of Culture and Tourism of the People's Republic of China, Public Service Division, *Letter of the Ministry of Culture and Tourism on Proposal No. 02028 of the Fifth Meeting of the 13th National Committee of the CPPCC (No. 164 in the category of Sports and publicity)* https://zwgk.mct.gov.cn/zfxxgkml/zhgl/jytadf/202211/ t20221117_937545.html

netizens – an internet penetration rate of 59.2 percent – with the urban-rural Internet penetration gap reduced to 19.1 percentage points.

To further support cultural revitalization, a national fitness campaign has been designed since 2017 to achieve the following goals: improve sports and fitness organizations; construct sports and fitness facilities; enrich sports and fitness activities; support sports and fitness events; strengthen physical fitness guidance; and promote sports and fitness culture. The campaign has reached all urban and rural areas, improving rural sports facilities, enhancing access to basic sports and fitness services, as well as accelerating the establishment of a public service system for sports and fitness. According to *the Statistical Communiqué of the People's Republic of China on the 2021 National Economic and Social Development,* there were almost 4 million sports venues in the country, covering a total area of 3.41 billion m^2 with per capita space of 2.41 m^2, providing rural communities with much-improved basic public sports facilities.

5.3.3 The quality of rural culture and sports services continue to improve

New management and operational mechanisms for delivering cultural services have been introduced, such as governments procuring public cultural services from the private sector. These reforms have contributed to innovation in public cultural services, expanding their variety and scope.

5.3.4 Traditional rural culture is being effectively passed on

Preservation and utilization of agricultural heritage has been strengthened. As of 2021, MARA has designated 138 items of agricultural heritage. Six rounds of fieldwork have been carried out to discover more of China's most important agricultural heritage sites, resultant in a steady increase in the number of such sites, with more diverse types, covering more regions and ethnicities. In particular, a number of traditional agricultural systems with unique characteristics in the central and western regions have been included in the scope of protection, showcasing a wider range of China's long and rich history of farming culture.

More efforts have been dedicated to protecting traditional villages. By 2021, the Ministry of Housing and Urban-Rural Development (MOHURD) had added 6,819 villages to the list of traditional Chinese villages in need of protection. These villages are managed under a nameplate system, in which basic village information and the name of the person responsible are inscribed on the plate for open and easy scrutiny. The measures serve as a model and have protected traditional villages from disappearing in 10 cities and prefectures. Digital museums of traditional Chinese villages have also been constructed. The number of villages with a digital museum has reached 606, covering 31 provinces, districts and cities. This has helped to reverse the rapid trend of traditional villages disappearing and strengthened the influence of traditional

Chinese culture. ①

Special Column 2: Chinese Farmers' Harvest Festival

After the launch of the rural revitalization strategy, China established the Chinese Farmers' Harvest Festival in 2018 as the first national festival dedicated specifically to the country's farmers. MARA and relevant departments are responsible for organizing numerous events, such as online and offline promotional events for agricultural products designed to increase rural incomes, along with a range of agricultural activities to enhance public knowledge and encourage engagement in Chinese agricultural traditions.

---

① Informaon Center, 2022, Tradional Chinese Village Digital Museum, *Traditional village weekly information highlights (05.16-05.22)* Retrieved from: http://www.dmctv. cn/zxShow.aspx?id=187

6

Ecological Revitalization

6.1 Significance of Ecological Revitalization

China's proposals for building an ecological civilization and achieving its dual carbon goals (reaching peaking carbon emissions before 2030 and carbon neutrality before 2060) have set an ambitious green tone for the country's future development. As society shifts increasingly towards the green transition, one of the major tasks for rural revitalization is to coordinate rural development with environmental protection. Ecological Revitalization consists of three main themes:

6.1.1 Achieving a green and low-carbon transition in agriculture to reduce the pressure of agricultural activities on the environment.

Agriculture is a major source of GHG emissions and a giant carbon sink system, yet at the same time it is a victim of global warming and climate change. Extreme weather events caused by climate change – such as hot spells, drought and flooding – threaten the healthy development of agriculture and the nation's food security. It is therefore necessary to promote a greener model of agriculture, enhancing the quality of agricultural products while reducing use of resources, in an environment with limited availability of arable land and water. This model can safeguard the nation's food security, create new development opportunities in the agricultural sector and stimulate green consumption at the same time.

6.1.2 Satisfying the people's demand, especially rural residents, for a pleasant living environment, promoting a healthy planet, and accelerating the building of a beautiful countryside. Compared with urban residents, Chinese rural residents generally enjoy a less livable environment, with significant gaps in sanitation facilities, particularly waste and sewage disposal services. As the economy develops, with urban and rural areas engaged in closer social exchanges, residents in both areas will have higher expectations for cleaner air and water, as well as a healthier environment.

6.1.3 Conserving and restoring rural ecosystems under the guidelines of China's ecological civilization, to enjoy the social, economic and ecological benefits of lucid waters and lush mountains.

6.1.4 Accelerating the Green Transition in Agriculture

China's "1+2+3" goal[①] involves controlling (1) overall water consumption for agriculture, (2) reducing the use of fertilizers and pesticides and (3) extensively utilizing animal manure and straw as resources, while recycling film mulch. These actions can help to establish a green agricultural system aligned with its carrying capacity in terms of resources and the environment, supporting the country's overall ecological goals.

---

① "China's '1+2+3' goals" were proposed by the Ministry of Agriculture at the national agricultural meeting in 2014, followed by a series of documents released by the MOA for implementing these goals, which have become the key task of green agriculture development during China's "13th Five-Year Plan" period.

6.2 Strengthening resource conservation and their sustainable use

Since the launch of the rural revitalization strategy, China has made great efforts to conserve arable land and use water efficiently in agriculture, with encouraging results in boosting green development in agriculture and building China's ecological civilization.

6.2.1 Achievements in conserving arable land

Through the *Action Plan on Conserving and Improving the Quality of Arable Land,* the country has specified goals on improving the quality of arable land, treating heavy metal contamination and plastic pollution. Technical measures have been taken to conserve and improve the quality of arable land, which have raised the quality of topsoil. These include developing prime farmland that is well-provisioned with facilities and amenities, conserving chernozem soils in northeast China, controlling soil pollution and managing soil rehabilitation, recycling straw on farmland, replacing chemical with organic fertilizers, practicing crop rotation and fallow systems[①], subsoiling[②] and deep plowing, along with treating heavy metal contamination. In 2021, around 67,000 km^2 of chernozem soil were under conservation and utilization. There has been a steady improvement in the quality of arable land. According

---

[①]　A fallow is a stage of crop rotation in which arable land is left without sowing for at least one harvest cycle. This can allow the land to recover, while disrupting pests feeding on the crop.

[②]　Subsoiling is a soil management technique to improve crop production, by loosening subsoil to reduce compaction.

to the national standard released in 2016, arable land in China is appraised by MARA every five years on a scale of 1-10, 1 being the best quality land. In 2014, the average rank was 5.11; in 2019 it was 4.76, an increase of 0.35 points.

6.2.2 Agricultural water use efficiency is improving steadily

China suffers from a serious shortage of water resources; the imbalance between supply and demand is a major challenge to its sustainable development. Placing a high value on saving water in agriculture, in 2012, the General Office of the State Council issued the *Outline of the National Agricultural Water Conservation Program (2012—2020)*. Following its guidelines, the Ministry of Water Resources (MWR) and MARA have promoted greater efficiency in the use of agricultural water resources. Their measures include building efficient water-saving irrigation facilities, such as field water pipelines, sprinklers and micro-irrigation in areas short of water, with inefficient irrigation, or with a prominent imbalance between supply and demand due to uneven temporal and spatial distribution, adapting to local conditions. The measures are expected to increase the scale and spread of effective irrigation, improve water utilization efficiency, as well as encourage intensive water conservation and use. In 2021, the effective utilization coefficient of farmland irrigation water reached 0.568, up by 0.052 from 2011.

6.3 Significant progress in preventing and treating agricultural nonpoint source (NPS) pollution

Propelled by strong policies such as the *Opinions on Comprehensively Enhancing Ecological and Environmental Protection and Resolutely Winning the Tough Battle for Prevention and Control of Pollution*, as well as the *Action Plan for the Battle of Agricultural and Rural Pollution Control*, the country has clarified its "1+2+3" goals through a strategy to prevent and control agricultural NPS pollution,[1] which has moved on from treating existing problems to curbing increments.

6.3.1 Use of chemical fertilizers is falling steadily

In 2015, the former Ministry of Agriculture rolled out the *Action Plan on Zero Growth of Fertilizer Use by 2020*, which made specific arrangements for improving the efficient use of chemical fertilizers to increase output and quality. Since 2016, the nationwide use of fertilizers and pesticides has decreased every year, reversing a long-standing upward trend. The volume of fertilizers used for crops across China fell by 13.8 percent, from 60.2 million tons in 2015, to 51.9 million tons in 2021 (See Figure 5).

---

[1] Nonpoint source pollution (NPS) comes from multiple points, such as excess fertilizers, insecticides and herbicides. It can spread through various means, including land runoff or drainage, with significant negative impacts on water quality.

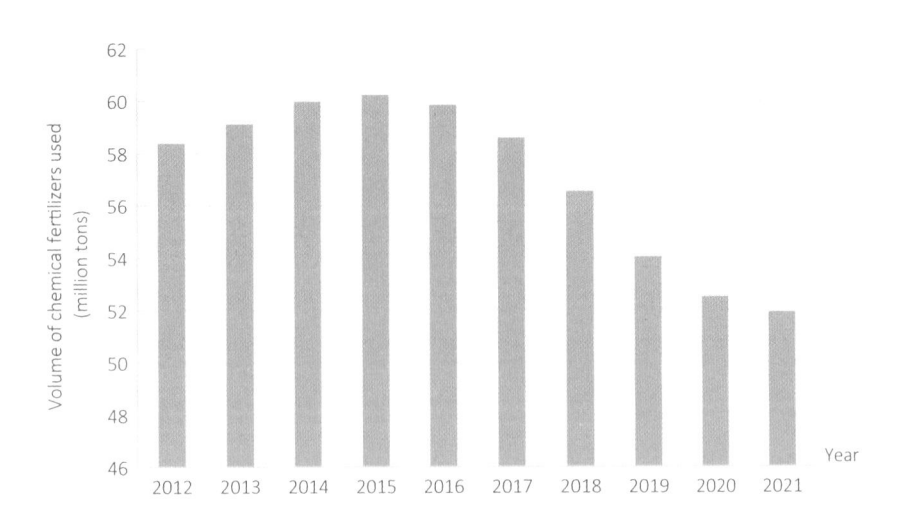

Figure 5: Volume of Chemical Fertilizers Used from 2012 to 2021

Source: China National Bureau of Statistics, Annual data on agriculture, https://data.stats.gov.cn/easyquery.htm?cn=C01

6.3.2 Use of pesticides continues to fall

In 2015 the former Ministry of Agriculture rolled out the *Action Plan on Zero Growth of Pesticide Use by 2020*, making specific arrangements to improve the efficiency of pesticide use. Under its guidelines, MARA has vigorously pushed forward actions to reduce the use of pesticides and improve their efficiency, as well as replaced chemical methods of prevention and control with green approaches. Specifically, 94 model counties have been established for green prevention and control, which promote green technologies for increased production. These include ecological, biological, and physiochemical traps and controls, bee pollination, along with the use of more efficient and less toxic biopesticides.

Voluntary agricultural technicians go to Fenghua Village, Tal Lake Town in the county to publicize agricultural knowledge.

Source of pictures:National Publicity and Education Center for Rural Revitalization

A training campaign on scientific and safe use of pesticides is also being carried out nationwide, helping millions of farmers and new agricultural operating entities to apply key technologies for reducing pesticides. As scientific pesticide application becomes more broadly accepted, pesticide-saving technologies are being more widely adopted, accelerating the use of green, efficient products. Highly-efficient and low-risk pesticides now account for over 90 percent of the total used. In 2021, the green pesticide utilization rates for three major crops across China – rice, wheat and corn – all exceeded 40%, 4-5 percentage points higher than in 2015.

6.3.3 Utilization of animal manure

Agricultural production inevitably produces waste, including animal manure from livestock and poultry farming, straw and plastic film used for crop protection. Unless treated properly, such waste will have a negative impact on the environment. Therefore, utilizing agricultural waste as a resource is an effective way to

develop a circular economy and achieve sustainable development. In 2016, the *Plan on Promoting the Pilot of Utilizing Agricultural Waste as Resources* was published, exploring effective technical methods and creating a comprehensive model of agricultural waste treatment through pilots.

In 2017, the General Office of the State Council published the *Opinion on Accelerating the Utilization of Waste from Livestock and Poultry Farming*[1], a campaign to encourage the use of animal manure as a resource and accelerate the green development of animal husbandry. Afterwards, the former MOA formulated the *Action Plan for Utilizing Animal Manure as A Resource*[2] *(2017—2020)* to activate key tasks. This created a system whereby the project is implemented across an entire county, supplemented by multiple measures, such as introducing organic fertilizers for fruit, vegetables and tea, as well as testing heavy metal residues. Under the guidance of the plan, all 585 major livestock counties have engaged in county-wide projects promoting animal manure as a resource. In 2020, similar projects were carried out in another 120 counties that are less livestock-oriented, to improve their capacity to treat and utilize animal manure. In 2021, the campaign yielded positive results: the national comprehensive utilization rate of animal manure exceeded 76 percent – 16 percentage points higher

[1] Public Information of the State Council of the People's Republic of China, (2017), *Opinion on Accelerating the Utilization of Waste from Livestock and Poultry Farming,* retrieved from,https://www.gov.cn/zhengce/content/2017-06/12/content_5201790.htm

[2] Public Information of the Ministry of Agriculture and Rural Affairs of China, (2017), *Action Plan for Utilizing Animal Manure as A Resource (2017-2020),* retrieved from: http://www.moa.gov.cn/nybgb/2017/dbq/201801/t20180103_6134011.htm

than in 2015 – and over 97 percent of large-scale breeding farms were equipped with manure treatment facilities.[1]

6.3.4 Comprehensive use of straw

To address challenges related to the surplus of straw, several measures have been adopted. MARA has identified 401 key counties across the country for work on straw use, with a focus on adopting straw as fertilizer, fuel, feedstuff, raw material and base material (the "five materials") . Secondly, the ban on straw burning was reinforced through more extensive use of technologies, such as remote sensing from satellites, drones and high-definition cameras to monitor and control ignition points, along with special inspections to enforce burning bans by holding offenders to account. The open burning of straw has diminished sharply. In 2021, more than 647 million tons of straw were recycled across the country, with their utilization rate reaching 88 percent[2] and an upward trend of using straw for the "five materials".

6.3.5 Reducing and recycling plastic film

Led by MARA, multiple ministries have collaborated in a campaign against "white pollution", by regulating the actions of agricultural film producers, sellers and users, holding each entity accountable for recycling discarded film, while guiding local governments to

---

[1] Public Information of the Ministry of Agriculture and Rural Affairs of China, (2022), A *Reply to the 0509 Proposal of the Fifth Session of the 13th National People's Congress,* retrieved from: http:// www.moa.gov.cn/govpublic/xmsyj/202208/t20220825_6407761.htm

[2] Institute of Agricultural Resources and Regional Planning, CAAS (2022). *China Agriculture Green Development Report*

promote standard soil films that improve their recyclability from the onset. They have also worked on a full-process regulatory system that covers the production, sales, usage and recycling of agricultural film. Through this full-process regulation, the recycling rate of film waste across China now exceeds 80 percent[1].

6.4 Actions continue to increase variety and quality of seeds and breeds, build brands and promote standardization

In March 2021, the General Office of MARA issued the *Action Plan on "Improving Variety, Quality and Brand and Standardizing" Agricultural Production*. This proposes actions to breed better varieties, improve product quality, as well as build brands and standardize production, to advance the green development of agriculture more broadly. Examples of actions taken by MARA include:

By the end of 2021, more than 13,000 national and industrial standards applied to agriculture, effectively covering the full production process of major agricultural products.62,000 agricultural products have been certified as green and organic, or granted a geographic indication (GI), The overall pass rate[2] of

[1] The Bureau of Environment and Resources, National Development and Reform Commission of the People's Republic of China, (2021), *Farmland "white pollution" prevention and control effect is obvious, the recycle rate of agricultural film is stable at more than 80%*, retrieved from: https://www.ndrc.gov.cn/fggz/hjyzy/zyzhlyhxhjj/202106/t20210628_1315403.html

[2] The pass rate is formulated according to the *Law of the People's Republic of China on Quality and Safety of Agricultural Products*.

◆ Cultivate better varieties

selecting new varieties, purifying and reinforcing local specialty varieties, breeding breakthrough varieties with high yield and quality, as well as building a number of breeding bases for prime seeds.

◆ Promoting high-quality agricultural production

promoting technologies and production methods, improving the environment in production areas, promoting green inputs and safe green veterinary drugs, as well as building a key indicator system for agricultural product quality.

◆ Strengthening the capacity to build agricultural brands

fostering renowned brands and a brand appraisal system, strengthening brand management and regulations, along with advocating brand marketing. In addition, MARA is reinforcing regulations on agricultural products, to promote safe, green and high-quality agricultural goods.

◆ **Advancing standardization of the entire industrial chain**
led by new agricultural operating entities, driven by cross-sectoral services and the agro-processing industry, facilitated by the intensive processing of agricultural products and supported by pilot projects in key areas.

agricultural products through quality and safety monitoring exceeds 97.6 percent.[1]

6.5 Steady Improvement in the Rural Living Environment

Enhancing the living environment of rural areas is a significant element of the rural revitalization strategy and "Building a Beautiful China". Since the strategy launched, departments in all regions have followed the action plan on rectifying and improving rural living standards. Lessons in achieving this were learned from a pilot program in Zhejiang Province – "Thousand Village Demonstration and Ten Thousand Village Rectification". These have created systems to ensure all tasks relating to the rural living environment are implemented, creating more than 50,000 villages with diverse forms and distinct features.

---

[1] Ministry of Agriculture and Rural Affairs Press Office (2021, December 28). *The Pass Rate of 2021 Routine Monitor of Agricultural Product Quality and Safety is 97.6%.* Retrieved from: http://www.jgs.moa.gov.cn/gzdt/jgjdt/202112/t20211228_6385798.htm

6.5.1 Domestic waste treatment is fully covered in rural areas

In 2019, the MOHURD supported local governments in implementing *the Guiding Opinions on Establishing and Improving the Collection, Transfer and Disposal System of Rural Domestic Waste.* By the end of 2021, more than 90 percent of villages in China were collecting, transferring and treating rural domestic waste, rising by 15 percentage points from 2017[①]. Localities generally adopt an approach under which waste is categorized by household, collected by village, transferred by town and disposed of by county. When local conditions permit, some rural areas are also integrated into the urban sanitation system. More than 95 percent of villages have carried out the clean village initiative, improving village living environments.[②]

6.5.2 Moving forward on rural domestic sewage treatment

In 2019, nine authorities – the Central Leading Group for Rural Work, MARA, MEE (Ministry of Ecological Environment), MOHURD, MWR, MOST, NRDC, MOF and CBIRC jointly issued the Guidelines on Promoting Rural Domestic Sewage Treatment. This directs localities to reduce sewage by category in a recycling-

---

[①] Policy document of Central People's Government of the People's Republic of China, (2022), *Interpretation of the Notice on Further Strengthening the Construction and Management of Rural Household Waste Collection, transportation and Disposal System,* retrieved from https://www.gov.cn/zhengce/2022-05/29/content_5692927.htm

[②] News Center of Ministry of Agriculture and Rural Affairs of the People's Republic of China, (2021), *The Central Agriculture Office and the Ministry of Agriculture and Rural Affairs notified and praised 106 advanced counties in the national village cleaning action* retrieved from http://www.moa.gov.cn/xw/bmdt/202102/t20210224_6362207.htm

oriented approach adapted to local conditions. MARA, NARR, MEE and other authorities have pressed ahead with developing rural domestic sewage discharge standards and a county-wide planning system. Rural domestic sewage treatment pilots have been conducted in 120 counties, with black and foul water bodies in rural areas broadly identified. By the end of 2021, China had built more than 500,000 rural domestic sewage treatment facilities, with almost 28 percent of domestic sewage in those villages now being properly processed[①].

6.5.3 The rural "Toilet Revolution" is making progress

Since 2018, toilet facilities in more than 40 million rural households have been upgraded. By the end of 2021, over 70 percent of rural households across the country had access to sanitary toilets. Of these, in the Eastern region, along with suburbs of central and western cities, 90 percent had access to sanitary toilets plumbed to harmless treatment facilities.

6.6 Good progress in building Rural Ecosystems

Since 2012, the Chinese government has made significant efforts to promote ecological civilization, proposing a strategy of coordinated management of mountains, water, forests, farmland, grassland and desert. A series of policies on environmental protection and

---

① News Center of Ministry of Ecology and Environment of the People's Republic of China, (2022), *a regular press conference of MEE in April, retrieved from: https://www. mee.gov.cn/ywdt/ zbft/202204/t20220422_975721.shtml*

restoration have been introduced. The implementation of supporting policies has strengthened the ecological functions of forests and grasslands, renewed wetlands, as well as protected and restored biodiversity. These include the *National Key Ecological Function Division (Revised Edition), the National Ecological Protection and Construction Plan (2013—2020), the Plan for National Grassland Protection, Construction and Utilization during the 13th Five-Year Plan Period and the Plan for National Wetland Protection during the 13th Five-Year Plan Period.* Such measures will further help to restore healthy ecological functions in rural areas.

One after another, beautiful highways have been built, opening up the door for impoverished areas to the outside world and creating a man-made miracle.

Source of pictures:National Publicity and Education Center for Rural Revitalization

6.6.1 Coordinated protection and restoration of mountains, water, forests, farmland, grasslands and deserts to enhance the resilience of ecosystems

China supports rural areas in coordinating all natural factors for the overall protection, systematic restoration and comprehensive treatment of mountains, water, forests, farmland, grassland and deserts, to improve the functioning of regional ecosystems and environmental quality.

a) Good progress in grassland protection and restoration

To protect grasslands, the supervision and inspection of the designation of prime grassland protection zones have been reinforced, farming-pastoral ecotones[1] (FPE) have been delineated and red lines have been set for prime grassland protection. The coverage of grassland vegetation in major ecological engineering zones is 11 percentage points higher than in other zones, while the grass is over 50 percent taller.[2] Meanwhile, in accordance with the policy on prime grassland protection, China continues to apply the allowance incentive for grassland protection and the program of returning pastures to grassland. Through grazing prohibition, rest-grazing, rotational grazing, captive breeding, grassland renovation and grass plantation, the grass to livestock ratio is improving. The transition of the grassland livestock industry from traditional, nomadic husbandry to modern husbandry, is also being facilitated.

---

[1] An ecotone is a transition area where two very different ecosystems meet.

[2] Ecological engineering zones are areas that the government has identified for restoration and protection, to improve ecosystem functions and services.

Areas of farmland returning to forest and grassland, as well as pasture returning to grassland, are expanding. By the end of 2020, the Fraction of Vegetation Cover (the fraction of ground covered by vegetation as a percentage of the totalarea) for grassland had reached 56.1 percent, compared to 54 percent in 2015[1].

b) A shelterbelt forest system[2] is in place

Under projects related to important ecosystem protection and restoration, six million hectares of forest are now under protection and a contiguous agricultural shelterbelt forest system has been established in major agricultural areas. Shelterbelt projects on the Yangtze River, the Pearl River and China's coastal areas, along with the Taihang Mountains, have received a total of RMB 1.87 billion (USD 280 million) from the central budget for construction tasks across 3,426 km^2 of land,supporting better natural resources in construction zones, higher quality forests and greater environmental security.

---

[1] News Center, Ministry of Agriculture and Rural Affairs of the People's Republic of China, 14, Jul 2021, *Agricultural modernization brilliant five-year series of publications XXIVhe ecological environment of grasslands across the country continued to improve:* Retrieved from: http://www.ghs. moa.gov.cn/ghgl/202107/t20210714_6371800.htm

[2] To tackle the severe problem of environmental degradation and the ever-increasing loss of natural resources, since 1978 the Government of China has started implementing the Three-North Shelterbelt Programme, namely the "the Great Green Wall", which is composed of the network of shelterbelts and tree plantations across the entire region in northern China. The Three-North Shelterbelt Programme is the largest afforestation programme in the world. It aims to establish 35 million ha of shelterbelt forests between 1978 and 2050.

6.6.2 Advances in protecting water resources and the ten-year fishing ban on the Yangtze River is beginning to have an impact

In 2020, MARA started a ten-year fishing ban across key waters along the Yangtze River, as well as on all the seven major inland rivers through a closed-season system. Major rivers, lakes and seas across China are all covered by the fishery ban and moratorium. To accelerate resettlement and support for fishers, the central government has allocated a subsidy of RMB 13 billion (USD 1.9 billion), with supporting funds of RMB 11.5 billion (USD 1.7 billion) from local governments, providing social security for 218,000 people and helping 165,000 to secure jobs in other industries.

Emphasizing the protection of rare or endangered species, China has carried out action plans for saving rare species, including the Chinese sturgeon, Yangtze finless porpoise and Yangtze sturgeon. It has also formulated the *Plan for Building Biodiversity Conservation Projects on the Yangtze River (2021—2025),* to further protect and nurture aquatic creatures along the Yangtze.

Organizational
Revitalization

7.1 Significance and Types of Rural Organizations

Revitalization of rural organizations andinstitutions is an important component of China's rural revitalization strategy. It refers to reinvigorating organizations in rural areas, allowing them to better perform their political, economic, social, cultural, environmental and other functions, so as to further strengthen rural governance. According to their functions, rural organizations in China can be divided into four types: political organizations, autonomous organizations, economic organizations and social organizations (Figure 7).

Historically, rural organizations in China have placed an important role on rural governance at village level, with evolving functions as rural areas developed. As distinct from urban organizations where functions are assigned to different organs, rural organizations have long played multiple roles. The Party branch committee and villagers' committee (collectively known as "two committees") at the level of the administrative village (potentially a number of distinct geographical villages) are organizations with overlapping functions, such as economic, political and social organizations.

Figure 7: Categories of Rural Organizations

Rural political organizations

Party groups, Party branches and general Party branches established in natural and administrative villages, as well as Party organizations built within other rural economic and social organizations, etc.

Rural economic organizations

Rural economic collectives, rural cooperatives, agricultural enterprises, family farms, agricultural socialized service organizations, etc.

Rural autonomous organization

Villagers' committees, villagers' groups, villagers' councils, village affairs supervision committees, etc.

Rural social organizations

Rural elderly care associations, women's federations, rural mutual aid cooperatives for poverty alleviation funds, various professional technical association, new-type rural opinion leaders' organizations, councils on wedding and funeral management, etc.

Source: Policy Documents of the State Council of the People's Republic of China, (2019), Regulations of the CPC on the Work of Rural Grass- roots Organization. Retrieved from: https://www.gov.cn/zhengce/2019-01/10/content_5356764.htm

Their membership is usually limited to a small group of people in a particular locality, or those engaged in a particular line of work, thereby establishing clear membership boundaries. The organizational structure also tends to be simple, due to limited membership turnover.

Box 2. Categories of Rural Organizations

a) Rural political organizations

Rural political organizations are the main rural grassroots organizations of the CPC. According to Regulations on the Work of Rural Grassroots CPC Organizations, they are responsible for "comprehensively leading all kinds of organizations and work in China's townships and villages",

including discussing and making major decisions on regional economic, political, cultural, social, environmental and Party matters, along with rural revitalization. In addition, village-level Party organizations are responsible for facilitating rural grassroots consultations on major decisions and supporting villagers in carrying out self-governing activities in accordance with the law.

Source of pictures:National Publicity and Education Center for Rural Revitalization

b) Rural autonomous organizations

Rural autonomous organizations, such as villagers' committees, are responsible for managing local affairs and representing the interests of their community. They serve as the major platform for rural people to directly participate in self-governing activities related to local political, social and economic life, such as building new village infrastructure and protecting their environment. Since the 1980s, China has established a system of village-level self-governance, which involves villagers' committees, villagers' meetings, villager representatives' assemblies and villagers' supervisory committees. They also provide a platform

for villagers to voice their concerns, providing decision-makers with extensive and timely information on public opinion in rural areas.

c) Rural economic organizations

Rural economic organizations are organizational units engaged in agricultural production and management for specific economic goals. With the advance of China's reform and opening- up, along with the further division of labor and industries in rural areas, new organizational models are constantly emerging, including family farm alliances, farmers' cooperative unions, industrialization consortiums and socialized service alliances, as well as enhanced profit-sharing mechanisms. Specifically:

Rural economic cooperatives: In China's rural areas, landis collectively owned and contracted by farmers for operation. Rural economic cooperatives are organizations formed by rural residents to jointly manage collective assets at the village level.

Specialized farmers' cooperatives are formed by farmers with a common interest or specialty to jointly manage and operate their economic activities and resources related to that. Such organizations provide sales, processing, transport and storage services, as well as technologies and information related to agricultural production and operations, based on household land contracting and operations. By pooling their resources, knowledge and expertise, members can

improve the quality and quantity of their production, reduce costs, as well as access markets and financing that might be difficult to realise individually, strengthening their market risk management.

Family farms are a new type of agricultural management entity, operated by family members as the main labor force, engaged in large-scale,

intensive, commercialized agricultural production and management, with agricultural revenues being their main income source.

Agricultural enterprises are profit-oriented organizations involved in production and management activities such as planting, animal husbandry, forestry, fishing and other agricultural industries. Thanks to their larger scale and reach compared to small-holder farmers, they possess advantages in integrating rural resources, such as land, labor, capital, culture and technologies.

d) Rural social organizations

Rural social organizations are nongovernmental or nonprofit organizations that play a vital role in rural socio-economic development, by serving as intermediaries, communicators and coordinators. They encompass a wide range of organizations, such as rural elderly care associations, women's federations, special technology associations, along with councils on wedding and funeral management.

Rural organizations are important entities that cover every aspect of rural development. Different organizations play different roles in rural revitalization. Economic organizations can unite small farmers and help them to build strengths in economic scale and resilience to market risks. Political organizations are key in attracting and fostering talented workers. Social organizations and self-governing organizations play a crucial role in cultural and Ecological Revitalization, by encouraging the rural population to protect cultural heritage, establish good rural ethics and conserve the environment. Consequently, to increase their capacity, the

government must strengthen relevant policies, encourage more talented people to work in those areas and allocate more funds to them.

7.2 Actions and Measures in Revitalizing Rural Organizations and Related Institutions

7.2.1 Strengthening self-governance with innovative forms of stakeholders' engagement

Since China's reform and opening up, rural self-governing organizations and their related institutions have continued to evolve.

Firstly, China's rural self-governing organizations have formed an organizational structure whereby executive, decision-making and supervisory responsibilities are separated and act as a check on each other. Their governance structure includes villager meetings and representative assemblies as the major decision-making bodies, the villagers' committee as the executive body and the village affairs supervision committee as the oversight body.

Secondly, community-level negotiations, along with village regulations and agreements are promoted. In addition, more self-governing organizations have emerged, such as villager and ethnic conferences, as well as anti-gambling and anti-drug associations.

Thirdly, China has promulgated *The Organic Law of the Villagers' Committees of the People's Republic of China* in 1998 and revised it in 2010. In 2002, 2004 and 2009, the General Office of the CPC Central Committee and the General Office of the State Council issued institutional documents on several critical issues including: ensuring smooth elections for villagers' committees, improving transparency of village affairs and strengthening democratic management systems. Over 640,000 villages and communities in China are equipped with professional legal advisors, accounting for more than 90 percent of counties in China.

Special Column 3:

Xiuzhou District in Zhejiang: Village Regulations and Agreements Cultivate New Cultural Customs

Village regulations and agreements are self-regulating rules formulated by villagers based on the local context, with the aim of maintaining social order, social public morality and village customs, which guide villagers'behavior. For the harmonious and civilized development of the village and its residents, the villagers' committee of Tengyun village, Xiuzhou District, Jiaxing city, Zhejiang Province, has formulated people-oriented regulations and agreements to explore new models of community-level governance in recent years.

In line with the rural revitalization strategy, the Tengyun Villager Committee has improved its village regulations and agreements about

marriage and family, along with neighborhood relationships, improving the local living environment and security with popular participation. One of the new agreements is to build a more pleasant village environment, by encouraging villagers to keep the locality clean, maintain green spaces, keep areas around their houses in order and sort garbage at source. Through such agreements, the committee is forming a new model of governance based on communal action and shared benefits, with a rewarding system for individuals and families that best follow regulations and agreements, while violators receive constructive criticism and education from the committee.

7.2.2 Boosted economic organization to take the lead

China consistently explores ways to develop the collective economy and cultivates new types of agricultural businesses, such as family farms, farmer cooperatives and commercial organizations that provide agricultural services. The No.1 Central Document issued by the Central People's Government every year regularly highlights the importance of new high-quality types of agricultural business. To this end, in 2022, MARA promulgated the *Notification of Improvement of New Types of Agricultural Businesses,* underpinning rural revitalization and the modernization of agriculture and rural areas.

By the end of 2021, official recognition had been granted to more than 90,000 enterprises as leading bodies in agricultural industrialization, as well as to 3.9 million family farms and 2.22

million farmers' cooperatives. Better benefit-sharing mechanisms also arose, such as contract farming, dividend sharing and equity cooperation, raising the incomes of rural residents.

7.2.3 Social organizations to provide better public services

To emphasize the value it places on rural social organizations, the CPC Party Committee and State Council introduced the *Opinions of the General Office of the CPC Central Committee on the Party Building of Social Organization (for Trial Implementation)* in 2015. It also released the Opinions of the Ministry of Civil Affairs on the Development of Community Social Organizations in 2020 and the *Opinions of the State Council on the Improvement of Management of Urban and Rural Communities* in 2021.

The State Grid Shaanxi Yulin Power Supply Company dispatched the first secretary of Lijiazhan Village, Shajiadian Town, Mizhi County, to discuss with the villagers the advantages of establishing a breeding cooperative.

Source of pictures:National Publicity and Education Center for Rural Revitalization

These regulate and refine guidelines for the development, management and supervision of rural social organizations. With

the support of national policies, rural social organizations – such as opinion leaders' councils[①] and volunteer associations – are playing a more important role in rural governance. For example, women's federations at community level take the lead in encouraging women to contribute to economic development, environmental protection, as well as managing rural customs and civic life. In addition, many social organizations promote projects that focus on female equality: the China Foundation for Rural Development and the Ant Foundation launched the Digital Heroine Mu Lan Project to develop county-level digital industries and new forms of professional training, creating more diverse employment platforms and opportunities for women in underdeveloped areas of central and western China.

Special Column 4:

Local Female Volunteers Safeguard the River Environment in Neixiang, Henan

At Pengying Village, Zuoqu Township, Neixiang County, Henan Province, a group of female volunteers are busy along the Ziqi River, a tributary of the Danjiang River, removing garbage, patrolling the waterway, removing weeds and deterring antisocial behavior. Their bright red waistcoats form a spectacular contrast with the green water plants.

This volunteer team of "water-guardians" was set up by female members of households that have been lifted out of poverty, along with "left-behind" women[①] in Pengying Village. They each spend about two days a week protecting brooks in the village and on the Ziqi River.

"I asked some women in the village to join me in the team. We can clear the garbage in the waters in our free time. In doing so, we hope to protect the river nearby and help all the villagers get access to clean water, " said Sun Xiaoying, the team leader, adding that team members help conserve the environment while socializing.

With the encouragement of Sun, her 24-year-old daughter, Yuan Yanting, also became a member of the team, which has grown to more than 10 women. Neixiang County is the source and catchment area, as well as the main water conservation area of Danjiangkou Reservoir and the key water source of the middle section of China's South-to-North Water Diversion Project. It is responsible for transferring water to China's northern areas. The Ziqi River in Pengying Village ultimately flows into the Danjiangkou Reservoir.

---

① "Left-behind" refers to children and other members of households who remain in their home villages while the family breadwinners travel elsewhere to work as migrants.

In addition to protecting these waters, the team also plays an important role in village governance, including improving the living environment, providing services for left-behind groups, assisting in nucleic acid testing and reminding residents to keep safe in the summer. They are always willing to help whenever and wherever they are needed.

Thanks to their efforts, the water of the Ziqi River has become clearer and the local environment more beautiful. Other neighboring villages are now following the example of Zuoqu Township. A "water-guardians" team has been established in Chenjiaying Village, with a voluntary service team in Wangjing Village. Both are composed of female residents and team members are making a difference in their residential environment and providing voluntary services for vulnerable groups in the community.

Chen Wanghui (first from left), director of the village committee of Maoshui Village, Dawei Town, Xiaojin County, Aba Tibetan and Qiang Autonomous Prefecture, Sichuan Province, led the masses to develop the rose planting industry and get out of poverty.

Source of pictures:National Publicity and Education Center for Rural Revitalization

Rural organizations are diverse. They include the Party, the market, self-governing organizations and social organizations with different priorities and functions. All have a role to play. Experience has shown that to revitalize rural organizations, China should strengthen the leadership of rural grassroots Party organizations and encourage autonomous organizations to participate fully in managing rural social affairs. It is also important to allow market-oriented organizations to play the main role in resource allocation, as well as leverage the vital functions of social organizations in gap areas out with the responsibilities of the government and market. This will result in positive coordination and interaction among the various entities involved.

Led by Party organizations, village committees can create favorable conditions for market organizations. Production allocation in agriculture and rural areas should be further optimized to effectively boost social organizations, promote social progress and create a strong force for revitalizing rural organizations.

Working across all stakeholders, it is possible to continue to improve quality of life, economic output and governance in the countryside – a crucial step in realizing the core promise of the SDGs: to end all poverty and leave no one behind.

翻转进入英文版阅读